KANSAS MUSIC

KANSAS MUSIC

STORIES OF A RICH TRADITION

Debra Goodrich Bisel

THE
History
PRESS

Published by The History Press
Charleston, SC 29403
www.historypress.net

Front cover, top center: Portrait of Count Basie, Aquarium, New York, New York. *Courtesy of the Library of Congress Music Division, William P. Gottlieb Collection*; bottom: Big Joe Turner in Hamburg, 1973. *By Heinrich Klaffs, licensed under CC BY 2.0.*
First published 2014

Manufactured in the United States

ISBN 978.1.62619.177.8

Library of Congress Control Number: 2014952379

This book is dedicated to the people who make the music carried by the South Wind and to those who hear it.

"Oh, I can still see the smiling faces
"When the times were so good
"Oh in the all familiar places
"I'd go back if I could
To the people of the south wind"

From "People of the South Wind"
Copyright © Kerry Livgren

CONTENTS

CONTENTS

FOREWORD

Deb Goodrich Bisel has a love for the state of Kansas, its stories, legends, people and history that is overarching and beyond compare. Her previous books for The History Press—*The Civil War in Kansas: Ten Years of Turmoil* and one coauthored with Michelle Martin, *Kansas Forts and Bases: Sentinels on the Prairie*—are about turbulent but definitive times in our nation's history. As a natural-born historian would, Ms. Goodrich Bisel saw untold stories that needed to be told and documentation that needed to be made. And so she did. As she stated for the *Topeka Capital-Journal*, "I'm a missionary for history. I convert people. That's my mission in life, to convert them to history."

Deb comes by her zealous nature honestly. Her father was a Baptist preacher in rural Virginia, where she was born and raised. Her birthright was a roots-oriented culture and history that was literally in the air: the early morning smell of mountain dew, the fragrant scent of bluegrass as she walked over it and the sound of bluegrass music on the radio. Stories and songs of family, friends and acquaintances rang in that same air, at once riveting and memorable. She found that she had an appreciation for people and what they had to say and, sometimes, sing and play. The connection was not only obvious but also inseparable. Her course was set, as was her love of the printed word. All of these things and so much more defined her upbringing. She was well aware of her vocation for history and journalism by the time she arrived in Kansas. A transplanted Kansan who instantly fell in love and stayed, she has "the fervor of the converted," as my mother would call it. She has a unique and insightful perspective that gives her occasion to see the vaunted Kansas sun shine in places where natives of the state, among others, might not.

It could well be said that *Kansas Music: Stories of a Rich Tradition* is her latest love letter to her adopted state. As a founding member and current president of the Kansas Music Hall of Fame, I am happy beyond measure that she chose to shine light on Kansas musicians, their stories, traditions and songs. I am equally happy to have her, a founding member of the Kansas Hall of Fame, as a difference-making and effective member of my own board of directors. She also graciously gave me a place in the book to write a brief synopsis about my parents, Louis and Betty Blasco. Their groundbreaking musical story will be told in greater detail in a forthcoming book of my own.

"Bloom where you are planted," as the saying goes. In so many ways, Deb Goodrich Bisel is the well-rooted, living and blooming embodiment of what is known as the Sunflower State. That she chose to stay in, make a life in, fall in love with and have her career in Kansas is indeed very fortunate, not only for the sometimes misrepresented and misunderstood state and its people, but also for its often untold and unheralded legacy worldwide. Kansas musical legacy is about to get a healthy dose of sunshine.

ALLEN BLASCO
President, Kansas Music Hall of Fame
September 2014

ACKNOWLEDGEMENTS

My profound thanks to my friends and reliable sources: Noel Coalson, Lisa Sandmeyer, Doug Ruth, Danl Blackwood, Michelle Martin, Cally Krallman, Diane Gillenwater, Kyler Carpenter, Chris Cruz, Bill Lee, Evan Johnson, Eric Bikales, Dennis LaPlant, Beth Meyers and the board of trustees and inductees of the Kansas Music Hall of Fame.

A very special thank-you to Sue Ann Seel, banjo-pickin' preacher woman, who brought music back into my life and is a good friend to me.

Thank you to the Kansas musicians whose music fills my days and nights with hope and fun and inspiration with just a spin on the CD player: Gary McKnight and True North, Riverrock, Scenic Roots, Greg Fox, the Free Staters, Chris Biggs, Eric Bikales, the Euphoria Stringband, Ray Hildebrand, Jimmy Dee and the Fabulous Destinations, Darryl Nickel, Judy Coder, Dan Kozak, Bridges, the Brazos Valley Boys, the Prairie Rose Rangers, Roger Weaver, Clayton Senne, Mike Finnigan, Cally Krallman, Pastense, Dan Crary, Josh Vowell, Finnigan & Wood. Thanks, too, to these "might-as-well-be-Kansans" Michael Martin Murphey, Jed Marum, Bryan Bowers, Mike Cross, Mountain Smoke and Connie Dover.

Thank you to all the businesses that make live music viable and thus turn an ordinary evening into an experience and to the guys and gals who host the jams and events. It is a lot of work that is done solely for the love of the music and the people who make it. A special shout out to Kyler Carpenter, Josh Vowell, Kenny Smith and Charlie Barber.

Thanks to the DJs who take music to a broader audience and offer entertainment and encouragement: Marshall Barber; Orin Friesen; Kim Murphree; Les Glenn; Jack Diamond; Bob McWilliams; Mike Hannah; and my *Around Kansas* co-host, Frank Chaffin.

Thanks to the music teachers and the music stores and especially Don McKenzie, Joel Edison and the very dear Rick Roberts.

Thanks to my editor, Becky Lejeune, who has the patience of Job; Julia Turner; and the staff at The History Press.

I cannot say enough kind words about the very talented Allen Blasco, who wrote the foreword and was always there for a word of encouragement or real help.

And finally, a very special thank-you to "Dixie Lee Jackson's House Band," Marc Houser and Borderline.

I love you all.

A MADE THING

This is a book about relationships. We flip on the radio, and a song comes on. Instantly, we are transported to another time, another place, and we recall what we were feeling, who we were with and who we wanted.

Like all art, music is a made thing. The process of making music is in itself beautiful and inspiring. In this endeavor, I am an observer, truly the reporter, for I possess no musical gifts except for a good ear. Having grown up with bluegrass, traditional and old-time music, where talent and quality cannot be faked, I know ability. And for that, I am most grateful. I really do not mind that this is a process in which I cannot participate; it is simply not my gift. But music inspires me to create in my own way, and that is what art is all about.

Many of my most inspired moments came in my living room when my former husband was having band practice. The room was spilling over with musical instruments: drums, guitars, bass guitars, mandolins, one banjo, keyboards, washboards, horns, flutes and a block of wood that he had tuned. Yes, it was a simple block of wood, and there was music inside it, just waiting for the right person to hear it.

When the idea of writing this book occurred to me, I was immediately struck by the interconnections of the musicians I knew. They were connected by family, work, bands, hobbies and hometowns, and each connection circled back to bring another circle in, until there was an absolute labyrinth

The band attached to Major General James Blunt was attacked and killed near Baxter Springs, Kansas, in 1863. Guerrillas under the command of William Clarke Quantrill were responsible for the massacre. *Author's collection.*

The Dodge City Cowboy Band put Cowtown on the map for something other than beef and Wyatt Earp. One of the most famous songs to come from the cowboy culture is the "Cowboy's Lament," or "The Streets of Laredo." Despite the name, it was inspired by an incident in Dodge City, Kansas, not Laredo, Texas. Frank Maynard claimed it was he who took the old Irish melody and adapted the words. Jim Hoy has edited and published Maynard's memoir, *Cowboy's Lament: Life on the Open Range. Author's collection.*

of connections. There are about three million people in Kansas. I have only met a couple million of them, but I am hard pressed to think of someone who is not involved in music or has a brother or sister or mate or child or dad who is a musician. Even my friend, General Richard Myers, fifteenth chairman of the Joint Chiefs (retired), plays a saxophone and has fond memories of band gigs during his college days at Kansas State.

With so much music and so many musicians, this book is not all inclusive. It only scratches the surface of all the talent and the great venues across the state. I hope there is enough of a sampling, however, for the reader to appreciate the vast musical contribution Kansans have made. Rather, this book is about what I know, who I know and the music and musicians that have touched my life. Fortunately for me, I know a lot of very good musicians in all genres of music. Since I serve on the board of the Kansas Music Hall of Fame, I am partial to that organization and to promoting its goal of recognizing musicians. Since it was founded in 2004, dozens of deserving groups and individuals have been inducted, and hundreds, if not thousands, more are waiting. Just listing the various awards and accomplishments of Kansas musicians would fill this volume, and it would only be a list. I have opted instead to share some stories in the hope that we will visit again someday and share more stories. I would very much like to hear yours.

Kansas music begins with the elements—earth, wind, water, fire. In Kansas, the greatest of these is wind. The wind has always been the driving energy of anything Kansas. The wind wailed and careened, whispered and whined and left no blade of prairie grass untouched. It has inspired the Kaw Nation, the European pioneers, American aviators and, finally, songwriters.

My older daughter, Karen Knox, was working in the Tel Aviv office of an international insurance company. As she dropped off paperwork at the front desk, the song "Dust in the Wind" came on the intercom. The young Israeli receptionist, who was not the most proficient in English, was singing along.

"Oh, do you like this song?" Karen asked.

"I love this song!" she replied.

Walking back to her own space, Karen met a co-worker in the hallway, a middle-aged man. He, too, was singing along.

"Oh, do you like this song?" she asked.

"I love this song," he responded.

"I've met the guy who wrote it," she said.

"Wow! No way!"

"Yes, way," she said. "It's Kansas."

Founding member of the band Kansas, Kerry Livgren, has been inducted into the KMHOF as an individual and a member of Kansas and White Clover. *Deb Bisel.*

"Dust in the Wind" by homegrown, namesake band, Kansas, is one of the most recognized and oft-played songs in the world: the distinctive guitar rifts echo the wind itself, ethereal, fleeting; the lyric, so, so simple, so timeless. This is a song about the wind blowing dirt, and it is epic.

Why?

Because it is Kansas dirt and Kansas wind.

Therein lies the magic.

PART I

Oh, Give Me a Home!

Little girl, where will you go
Walking down an endless road
Don't you know you're far from home
Is that dog gonna keep you from feeling alone
What were you running from
Your stories just begun
We miss you in Kansas

From "We Miss You in Kansas"
Copyright © 2012 Marc Houser

I

THE CROOKED ROAD

Before there was an official designation, the Crooked Road was my home. My path was Willis Gap Road, clinging to the side of the mountain and crossing the Blue Ridge Parkway at milepost 192 between Orchard Gap and Groundhog Mountain. (The steepest part of the road was unpaved until a few years ago; for years, we terrorized tourists by driving up that road, stopping and pointing out the place where the bulldozer fell off the mountain when they tried to pave it.) From the nearby Parkway overlook, you can see Mount Airy, North Carolina, the home of Andy Griffith and the inspiration for the fictitious Mayberry depicted in the television show. You can see Pilot Mountain, the actual mountain, and a couple of landmarks from the town at its foot. This became the town of Mount Pilot on the Andy Griffith Show. The odd formation that Indians referred to as a "pilot," or guide rock, must have been too much to explain to a television audience. European settlers referred to it as Mount Ararat, and eventually the river that flowed past it was called the Ararat as well. Two communities along the river's course took the name Ararat because of this landmark—one in North Carolina and one in Virginia. I grew up on the Virginia side attending Blue Ridge Elementary School, where the windows framed the foothills where the creeks and branches came together to make that river. It wound its way through Surry County on the North Carolina side and poured into the mighty Yadkin River that flows into the Pee Dee and, eventually, the Atlantic Ocean.

Across the mountain, past Hillsville and Galax, is the tiny town of Fries, Virginia (pronounced Freeze). My grandma Coalson grew up there, and lots of aunts, uncles and cousins lived there or in nearby Independence. The Norfolk and Western train tracks hugged the New River and Grandma's stories of her childhood adventures lit my imagination. The New River flows north and west, through the deep gorges of West Virginia, before reaching the Ohio, then the Mississippi and, finally, the Gulf of Mexico. When we talked of "going to the river" as children, we were talking about the New. We camped and fished and imagined.

Geography shapes everything. The Scots-Irish settled into these hollows where a sane man would not have gone. Those pioneers brought their warrior ethic, their independent nature and their music. The music permeated everything, and there was no craggy nook beyond its reach. Our lives had a soundtrack—fiddle, banjo, guitar, mandolin. My summer nights were spent on the front porch watching the limbs of the willow sway in the moonlight while Grandpa leaned back in his straight-back chair and picked tunes on his banjo. The whippoorwill's song was his only accompaniment.

In the mornings, we woke to the scratchy reception of WPAQ radio with Flatt and Scruggs; the Stonemans; the Carter Family; the Stanley Brothers; Jim & Jesse; and the father of bluegrass himself, Bill Monroe. On Saturday mornings, the WPAQ Merry-Go-Round hosted by Clyde Johnson featured local bands. Cousins, neighbors, churchgoers—some came into Studio B spit-shined, donning matching suits, and others stumbled in, hung over from the Friday night frolic. I was there myself once, a second-grader in Miss Agnes King's Rhythm Band. I played the triangle, out of time. In some tragic cosmic accident, I inherited no musical ability except an ear. I can flatfoot (something akin to clogging for those of you unfamiliar with the term), but lots of folks can out dance me (my aunt Emma Lee to name one). I don't play an instrument, and I don't sing, except for Old Baptist hymns.

It seems odd when I explain it to people in Kansas. Daddy was a preacher, Primitive Baptist—or Old Baptist, as some of the members referred to it. He served churches from the mountains to the coast. The Primitive Baptist denomination dominated the mountains, their Calvinistic doctrine reflecting the independent spirit of mountain folk, folk who were music-makin', music-lovin', flatfootin' predestinarians. "What will be, will be" is the mantra. At some point, the church split over exactly how absolute predestation is. I grew up with the Hardshells, the absolutists. All others were "soft" on that doctrine and were on the "soft side." The churches were plain, having no steeples or adornment.

The church did not allow graven images (no pictures of Jesus on the wall), Sunday school (you do not learn faith, it is revealed to you) or, oddly, musical

Stephen Golightly on fiddle, Jim Krause playing bottle, Christina Floyd and Don Mycue in back in 1983. Doug DuBois invited musicians to camp out at the old schoolhouse in Climax, Kansas. Doug brought recording equipment, and a cassette tape was produced of the music recorded over the weekend. The following year, 1984, he did it again at a country place north of Lawrence, and another cassette was produced. Steve runs Alfred Packer Band. (Doug was a founding member in late '70s along with founder Jim Brothers, sculptor.) *Bayliss Harsh.*

instruments. The hymnbooks contained only lyrics, and the tunes were passed down from one generation to the next like quilts. Often, the preacher, or whoever led the singing, "lined" the songs, saying the line and then having the congregation sing it. Mostly, the singing was in minor keys. I remember that when one of the church ladies was asked why there was no music in our church, she replied, "There is. Not everyone can hear it." With no talent and no range, I can still hear the music, and I can sing some of these old songs. Obviously, that was all I was meant to sing.

Mama and Daddy both had pretty voices. At home, Mama sang those hymns while she washed dishes, but she also sang secular Christmas carols, old Irish ditties and some western swing and cowboy songs. Sometimes, she would pause long enough while doing the dishes to flatfoot when something particularly inspiring came on WPAQ. She could also yodel, quite well. Daddy desperately wanted to play an instrument, though not desperately enough to practice. He often came home from work and picked up an autoharp, sat in front of the TV and strummed no particular melody. Just strummed, and it was not unpleasant. He could actually play a little on the mouth harp when he wanted to. He liked western movies and cowboy songs, too, and in his dreams, he was probably Roy Rogers.

In my dreams, I was Lois Lane. I watched *Superman*, *Donna Reed* and *Leave It to Beaver*, and Lois Lane was the one woman who had an adventurous life. By the time I was fifteen, I was a reporter for the *Enterprise* in Stuart, Virginia, and later on, I wrote some stories for the *Bull Mountain Bugle*, as well. The big time came when I went to work for the *Mount Airy News*. Then I headed over to WSYD to work as a disc jockey and in sales. I was terrible at both, but so impressed was WPAQ's station manager that I could write and talk he offered me the job as news director at that fine establishment. Other than a real understanding of what constituted news, I was wholly unqualified. Like everything else, I learned on the job. While there, I formed a friendship with the morning DJ, Sherry Boyd, and we became roommates for a time and shared some musical adventures. (She emcees bluegrass festivals all over the country and now works with WPAQ's sister station, WBRF, in Galax, Virginia.) Our time together in that storied place is precious to me.

WPAQ is legendary in traditional music circles. The greats performed and/or recorded there: Charlie Monroe, Grandpa Jones, Little Jimmy Dickens, Del Reeves, Ralph Stanley, Lester Flatt and Earl Scruggs and Mac Wiseman, to name just a few. Sherry said that when the late John Hartford was in town for a show he asked her to pick him up and take him to the

The Free Staters returned to the stage at Lincoln Days in 2014. Jon and Betsey Goering founded the band in 2003 because, said Becky, no one else was doing music from the Territorial Era. *From left to right*: Ryan Mackey, Jon Goering and Betsey Goering. *Deb Bisel*.

station just so he could be in the same hallowed studio where many of his idols had played.

The Saturday morning show that owner/founder Ralph Epperson began in 1948, the "Merry Go Round," is one of the oldest, continuously running radio shows in the nation. ("The Grand Ole Opry" is the oldest according to my sources.) One Saturday, there was the usual "Merry-Go-Round" party atmosphere when Mike Seeger walked in the door. Pete's younger brother was a far bigger celebrity to us. He and his former wife, Alice Gerrard, along with Andy Cahan and Paul Brown, had toured the college campuses of America with Uncle Tommy Jarrell, the most famous of the old-time fiddlers. To Uncle Tommy's modest home in Toast, North Carolina, pickers flocked like pilgrims to learn tunes and tuning handed down in the mountains for generations.

Mike was unique in a genre that was itself unique. Having grown up in a well-educated family with broad exposure to many cultural influences, he was, as was his more famous sibling, drawn to the working class, to roots music. He respected its practitioners, whether blues, old-time or traditional, and was never arrogant of his own gifts. His band, the New Lost City Ramblers, influenced countless musicians and introduced thousands to music they had never heard. That evening, he and Paul Brown came to Reuben's Red Lantern in Fancy Gap, Virginia, for the square dance, and Mike asked me to show him my particular flatfootin' steps because he was working on a documentary. It was one of the more self-conscious moments of my life, and I am grateful he was enough of a gentleman not to comment on how star-struck I was. Since then, I have interviewed some pretty important people; none ever affected me as much as Mike Seeger.

I left WPAQ because my sister Denise and I had decided to start our own publication, *A Comin' and A Goin'*. Our office was located at the intersection of U.S. 52 and the Blue Ridge Parkway in Fancy Gap. The focus of our little foray into publishing was the music and culture of the Appalachian Mountains, basically, an excuse to do what we wanted to do anyway—hang out and listen to music. We had no clue what we were doing, but I would not trade that experience for the world.

In 1992, I moved to Kansas. I had never finished college, and I was going to attend Washburn University, earn a degree and return home. As is often the case, life had other plans, and here I am, not only a transplanted Kansan but also an evangelizing Kansan! I fell in love with the state's history and then its music.

You never know where a crooked road will take you.

2

HONEST WORK

When I moved to Kansas in 1992, my two favorite places were the Historic Topeka Cemetery and the Classic Bean, a coffee shop on Kansas Avenue. Each morning before work was spent with a rich latte engaged in stimulating conversation with local businessmen and attorneys. On Tuesday evenings, the Classic Bean featured open mic poetry hosted by Marshall "Harsh Marsh" Barber. Marshall bears a striking resemblance to Dr. Emmett Brown of *Back to the Future* fame and is just as expressive and bright. He hosted an oldies radio show where his knowledge of trivia and understanding of what makes music good combined for a Friday night worth sitting home for—except, there was also a jam at the Classic Bean on Friday nights. John Henderson, local mandolin player, sang a song that has resonated with me to this day and connected me to the musicians in my adopted state. Todd Rundgren's "Honest Work" has been likened to an Irish lament:

> *I'm not afraid to bend my back*
> *I'm not afraid of dirt*
> *But how I fear the things I do*
> *For lack of honest work*

Every musician has a "signature song," his or her own or a cover of something he or she does particularly well. When John shows up at the local watering holes, he is invariably asked to do "Werewolves of London," and it

Above: (Left to right) Danl Blackwood, Wendy Senogles and John Henderson perform at the Celtic Fox. *Doug Ruth*.

Opposite: Ric Barron performs the national anthem for the Kansas Hall of Fame ceremony at the Great Overland Station. Honorees that year included Ed Asner and Nancy Landon Kassebaum Baker. *Danl Blackwood*.

is killer! For me though, his signature song will always be "Honest Work." It speaks to my soul as, said John, "it speaks to me also, and every working-class mother's son."

John and Joel Edison had convinced Juliann Earl, who, along with her husband, Doug Thomas, owns the Bean, that Friday nights the bistro should stay open after 5:00 p.m. and host an open jam. That was my introduction to live music in Kansas. The best of local talent wandered in and stayed the evening.

"Kenny Smith," John continued. "Yes, he was there. And David Yount, Dan Brock, many more. We had twenty guitar players at a time."

"It was a horror show," he joked. "Lawyers, clerks, downtown workers, they all came." John added that the regional favorite the Cows was born of those jam sessions, and they are as energetic as ever, twenty years later.

It was that jam and clique of poets that took me to P'ore Richards across the street, and that is where I discovered Johnny I and the Receders. From

there, it was the Vintage Restaurant and Lounge, where the Solohogs regularly performed. These groups played popular music, rock 'n' roll classics and standards. They possessed very different styles, but the commonality was the talent and quality.

One of my favorite restaurants was Rosa's on East Sixth Street. I was not alone. Finding a seat at lunch, you would have thought they were giving away $100 bills. It was an intimate setting. Often, you found yourself sharing condiments with complete strangers reaching over your shoulder. A large, intense guy was often waiting tables. He was a personality who filled the room. He smiled at you insistently and could have coaxed a response from Ebenezer Scrooge. My friends whispered that he was with the Exceptions. The Exceptions. Wow. He was so intense serving the suicide burrito, I was almost afraid to go hear him sing. Years later, Ric Barron and his equally talented wife, Marta, are two of my dearest friends, and I don't believe I have ever heard a singer with such absolute control of his voice. And yes, he is still intense.

My link to the culture and music I had left behind was the *Flint Hills Special*, the weekly radio show hosted by Bob McWilliams on Kansas Public Radio. That show evolved into *Trail Mix*. In 2014, Bob was given the "Spirit of Folk Award" at the Folk Alliance conference in Kansas City, citing his work with both *Trail Mix* and *West Side Folk*.

"I felt huge gratitude," said Bob.

It was well-deserved recognition for decades of promoting traditional music. He took the time to write down some thoughts about how it had all started:

Starting in, I think, 1970, KANU FM in Lawrence had a bluegrass show (the first one was started and hosted by the great guitar player Dan Crary when he was in graduate school at KU). At some point by the late '70s, that had become a Sunday night show called the Flint Hills Special *(a take on the name of an Earl Scruggs tune, "Flint Hill Special," with a Kansas twist). When I started working at KANU in 1983, that show was co-hosted by Mike Allen and Rick Desko, with a bit of help on occasion from Dick Powers. The show's focus was bluegrass but with some time devoted to Celtic music, old-time music and traditional folk and a very small amount to contemporary folk. By the late '80s, Rick Desko had moved to Colorado, and Dick Powers became the co-host with Mike Allen. And in a couple of years, Mike left, and I became the co-host with Dick Powers.*

*I thought, however, that there should also be a show that had a focus on contemporary folk and singer-songwriters, which had very little exposure on KANU or other radio stations in the area. So I proposed a new show that would have that focus. After a lot of time and effort in honing the concept of the proposed show—and even more in choosing the name—*Trail Mix *debuted as a two-hour Sunday afternoon show from 2:00 to 4:00 p.m. At that time, KANU aired* Thistle and Shamrock *in the 1:00 p.m. hour, so the decision was made that about the first half hour of* Trail Mix *would focus on Celtic music, and then it would transition to contemporary folk and singer-songwriters. Some of the artists featured in the first few weeks were the likes of Cheryl Wheeler, Shawn Colvin, David Wilcox and Iris DeMent—and an artist who had just that spring released her first CD, Dar Williams. For several years,* Trail Mix *continued in that time slot with that focus while I continued to co-host the* Flint Hills Special *from 7:00 p.m. to midnight on Sunday nights. But at some point circa 1997–1998 (sorry I can't be more precise), after the departure of Dick Powers to focus on* *his new career in teaching and after a few months of me hosting the* Flint Hills Special, *the station made the decision to end the* Flint Hills Special *and to make* Trail Mix *a six-hour show, from 1:00 p.m. to 7:00 p.m., with bluegrass, old-time music and traditional folk folded in, and to make it more of a real "mix by not segregating the various styles into their own hours." In the twenty years since* Trail Mix *debuted, listener support during funding drives has grown very significantly, and especially after the move to the "new" radio station building with a great performance studio, there have been many terrific artists performing for* Trail Mix *in the KPR studio (including, among many others, Dar Williams, Tim O'Brien, John Gorka, Darrell Scott, Lucy Kaplansky, Eileen Ivers, Dervish and, from our own area, the likes of the Wilders, Connie Dover and Kelley Hunt). Many artists (and booking agents) have told me they played in Lawrence and this area because their music was being played on* Trail Mix *on Kansas Public Radio.*

At the time Trail Mix *started, my wife and I had started, a few months before, hosting house concerts in Lawrence. In 1996, I was approached about doing a concert series that would be held at West Side Presbyterian Church. I helped put together a concert featuring Lawrence's own Kim Forehand, and that led to the formation of a nonprofit organization, West Side Folk, to present folk (broadly defined) concerts here in Lawrence. While a ministry change at West Side Presbyterian Church three years later would lead to the series being presented in other venues, we decided to keep the name West Side Folk. Over these eighteen years, West Side Folk has presented a wide range of concerts, with a focus on singer-songwriters but also including bluegrass, old time, Celtic and traditional folk, in venues ranging from Liberty Hall to the Lawrence Arts Center (both the old and new one), the Lied Center Pavilion, Plymouth Congregational Church and, for the last few years, Unity Church of Lawrence. A sampling of the artists presented by West Side Folk would include Greg Brown, Dar Williams (both on her own and as part of Cry Cry Cry with Lucy Kaplansky and Richard Shindell, and we have also had a number of shows featuring each of the latter), Tim O'Brien and Darrell Scott (together and on their own), Dougie MacLean, Red Molly, Cheryl Wheeler, John Gorka, Susan Werner, Laurie Lewis, Dan Crary, Andy M. Stewart, Beppe Gambetta, Kelley Hunt, Greg Greenway, Carrie Newcomer, Tony Furtado, Dave Carter and Tracy Grammer, Ellis Paul, John McCutheon, Catie Curtis, Alasdair Fraser and Natalie Haas, Chris Smither, Bill Morrissey, the Lynn Morris Band, Small Potatoes and many others. I was told by people who began the Birdhouse series at the Manhattan Arts Center that they were inspired*

to do so by the example of West Side Folk and ditto for the formation more recently of the Last Minute Folk series in Topeka.

"So people tell me that between *Trail Mix* and the West Side Folk series, that I have played a big part in making the folk scene much more vibrant in northeast Kansas," Bob concluded. "If so, then that makes me very happy."

In 2008, I hosted my own radio show, three hours of talk each weekday on KMAJ AM. During that fifteen hours a week, military experts, authors, politicians, chamber of commerce promoters, scientists, actors, artists and musicians trekked to the studio or called in from afar. Having live music in the studio was the best. Getting those creative people to sit down for a conversation and sometimes even play a tune—these were the greatest rewards of a career in radio. There were call-in interviews with William Lee Golden of the Oak Ridge Boys and Vicki Lawrence ("The Night the Lights Went Out in Georgia" and Carol Burnett fame) prior to their concert appearances. There was an in-studio interview with Jim Malcolm, the troubadour from Scotland, a guest of Ian Hall, our own transplanted Scot.

One of the most unforgettable days was with Clayton Senne. He might have still been a teenager, I do not recall. Clayton brought his guitar and his

Opposite: Clayton Senne and his mom, Marta Barron. *Courtesy Marta Barron.*

Left: Morey Sullivan performs with the Junkyard Jazz but has been the lead singer for Hank Thompson's Brazos Valley Boys for years. *Deb Bisel.*

manager. When he played and sang, I forgot all about the listening audience. Shivers really did shoot up my spine. With a musical family—mom, dad and stepdad, all respected musicians—Clayton had no choice but to be talented. But the energy! I was not prepared for the incredible energy that came from that young man. Later on, he competed on the *X Factor* and was only one or two contestants away from making it to the television show. They should have picked him.

Others who were friends or would become friends were guests on my show: Cally Krallman, Diane Gillenwater, Tom Krebs, Joel Edison, Morey Sullivan, Jed Marum, Shannon Reilly with Topeka Civic Theatre, symphony conductor Dr. John Strickler—such a variety of talents and passions.

The depth and diversity of the talent in Kansas is simply staggering.

A Tale of Two Wives

By Ian Hall

Two Nazareth stories, in two separate continents, with two different wives...

Nazareth is a Scottish rock band from Dunfermline, usually associated with the worldwide hit "Love Hurts," from the 1975 album *Hair of the Dog*. I remember the band's albums as a teenager at Greenhall High School, just ten miles south of Edinburgh (maybe twenty-five miles from Dunfermline). It was our local band, no matter what Bay City Rollers fans said. I still remember the album covers—*Razamanaz*, *Loud and Proud*.

Years later, in the early '90s, Nazareth played a community center in Cowdenbeath, just ten miles from its home base, and I went along with my first wife. I looked forward to hearing the hits, but I did have a hidden agenda.

A few months earlier, BBC had done a cool series on various Scottish towns, and Nazareth had done a version of "Long Black Veil" in the closing credits. In the show, the members sang a capella, with only drums as their accompaniment, each band member beating some kind of rhythm.

I waited through the first half of the concert; then they had a break. We all went to the makeshift bar. To our surprise, the band also joined the fans, drinking their beers, standing in a small circle, being ignored by most of the audience, most being far too star-struck to intrude into their circle.

Not me. "I'm going to ask them where I can get a recording of it," I said to my first wife, who, to her credit, tried to hold me back. But it was too late; I was off, weaving through the groups. My target? The band.

"Hey guys," I said quite nervously. I mean, they were Nazareth. But to my surprise, I was welcomed into the circle with smiles and chinks of our glasses. "I have a question."

"What's up man?" Dan McCafferty croaked at me.

"You guys sang on a BBC documentary."

"Yes we did!" the band enthused. "'Long Black Veil,'" they chorused.

I knew I was close to my goal. "So what album is it on?" I asked, and that threw the cat in with the pigeons. They couldn't decide; they suggested various albums and then shook their heads, amicably arguing among themselves.

"We've never recorded it," McCafferty finally said. "Do you want us to play it tonight?"

Well, what could I say? They asked my name, and I left them to their beers.

In their second half, after a heavy rock song, they all kind of drifted off their instruments and shuffled to a line on the stage. One by one, they picked up drums, some unscrewing them from the drummer's kit. "We're going to do a request." Dan said, "One we've never done on stage before." The crowd cheered. I stood in awe, hoping that they'd go through with it. "This is the 'Long Black Veil.'"

They began a slow dirge beat, then as Dan McCaffrey stood to the microphone, he said, "This one's for Ian."

I felt chuffed and stood in the audience smiling throughout the performance.

I next bumped into Nazareth in Kansas City early in the next millennium. The local radio announced a concert in a kind of seedy part of Kansas City, and the race was on. "Let's go," my second wife said. "It'll be fun. They're your countrymen."

I have to be honest, I'd been drinking through the Saturday afternoon, so I couldn't drive. I nodded my consent, although I didn't relish the hour drive from Topeka to KC. But I nodded and got in the car. I mean, what else does a good husband do?

Well, we'd left it pretty late, and it was dark when we got into the area of the bar in question. Karla seemed to have an inherent idea of where she was going, and eventually, we

Ian Hall (pictured), a man of many talents, at the Kansas City Renaissance Festival, where he and his wife, Karla, operate Thyme2dream. *Courtesy Karla Hall.*

pulled into a packed parking lot, just as the band got out of their large bus.

"We're going to be late!" I yelled, but no matter what we did, no matter what route we took, we couldn't beat the band to the door.

I walked in right behind Dan McCaffrey, and the doorman put up his hand at my attempted entrance. "There's a cover charge!" he shouted.

"Thank God, we're not late." I said, out of breath from our run across the parking lot. "I just traveled five thousand miles to see these guys!" I joked. "They're from my home town!"

To our surprise, the last man from the band turned around, hearing my accent. "Where are you from?" he said in a heavy

Scottish accent. I swear it was Dan McCaffrey, but like I said, I had been drinking.

"Fife," I shouted, laughing at the irony of the situation.

"They're with the band!" he said, waving us inside, challenging the doorman to take money from us. Heck, my accent had got me another freebie.

They didn't play "Long Black Veil" in the seedy bar in eastern Kansas City, but we had fun. We'd gotten in free, and my notoriety had increased a notch.

Today, I looked up "Long Black Veil," and found Wikipedia's listing: "A version by Scottish rock band Nazareth was never released on an album, but is played at live concerts." Perhaps I contributed to rock history.

Now, the story of the second wife.

How we met is not the most original story, but quite sweet in its own way.

Sitting in Scotland, I was in a Yahoo chat room chatting about science fiction and science fantasy books with four or five other people, and on the screen comes this line: "I'm six foot three."

Well, I went, "Six foot three, so am I!" So I clicked on this person's profile page, and it turned out to be a woman. I wrote her a personal message, "So I could look you right in the eyes then."

"Yes, you could." Karla answered after a while.

I asked what type of stuff she was into, and she wrote back, "Scottish folk music."

I just about jumped off my seat. You see, I was a Scottish folk musician, singing in my own band Tandragee.

I remember being quite impressed with her knowledge of Scottish folk music, and of course, I did nothing to beat myself down. I had played the folk clubs in Scotland and either knew or had shared a stage with some of them.

She originally took six years off her age but soon came clean as our friendship developed. We were only three years apart.

KTWU's Lee Wright (left) a folk singer and songwriter in his own right, appears with Peter Yarrow of Peter, Paul and Mary. *Alice Eberhardt Wright.*

I made Karla a demo tape of the typical songs I sang, with a bit of explanation between the songs, and sent it off.

Of course, with the content and accompanying accent, I became an instant hit with her.

It wasn't long before we were arranging a flight for me, and we met in the arrivals lounge at KC International Airport. Well, of course, it turned out that the British army measured me at six foot two and a half, and rounded up. Karla, perhaps in an attempt to be demure, had rounded down. She was a full inch taller.

I met her father, Lee Wright, a renowned folk singer from Topeka, and even performed with them on my first trip. It seemed I was about to join a very musical family.

I moved over permanently two years later, in 2001, and we soon started singing together, at first as a new version of Tandragee, but later as Glenfinnan, in an effort to have a Scottish name that no American could misspell.

Glenfinnan has had many incarnations, but even today, fourteen years later, we still sing and play together. I play guitar, bodhran and whistle; Karla plays guitar, mandolin and bouzouki. Flint Goodrich plays fiddle. We usually have a drummer, sometimes a bass player and at times a piper. It's always fun.

That day that I met Karla online, I could have gone to any of twenty chat rooms. Neither one of us was really looking for someone. She wasn't there to chat up guys, and I wasn't there to chat up girls. It was pure luck, kismet or divine intervention—we'll never know, but we certainly have our suspicions.

3

JAM4DAN

Belief in our kids….belief in tomorrow….belief in music.

Jam4Dan is an annual benefit concert held every Martin Luther King Jr. holiday weekend at the Celtic Fox in Topeka. It has become Topeka's signature three-day musical event. It honors the late musician and teacher Dan Falley. The event raises scholarship funds to give Shawnee County youths an opportunity to further their musical studies and provides Topeka's musicians a unique opportunity to come together to share their love of music.

The first Jam4Dan was organized in January 2008 to help Dan's family meet its obligations after Dan died in a car accident north of Topeka. To say that he was beloved by the community is an understatement. His former bandmate drummer John Wooten commented, "Dan Falley was an inspiration to all who were blessed enough to observe him play his guitar. He was a kind gentle soul who'd give you the shirt off his back should you find yourself in need. During a band practice at his guitar shop one Friday evening I witnessed him hand over sets of strings to a musician who had no money but was in need of strings for a gig he had booked that evening."

"Dan had a heart of gold," continued John. "Mr. Dan Falley…I miss you buddy!"

The mood of that first event was somber, given the passing of a man whom many had called friend and who had influenced the Topeka music scene since the late '60s. As folks poured in and the musical intensity swelled, it became apparent, however, that there was good to be drawn from misfortune.

Above: (Left to right) Preston Miller, Alan Lawton, John Wooten on drums, Dave Houser and Marc Houser stand on stage for Jam4Dan6. *Doug Ruth*.

Left: Guitarist Dan Falley was a teacher and musician who was killed in car crash in 2008. The Jam4Dan began as a way to help the family with expenses and turned into an annual event to raise money for music scholarships. *Doug Ruth*.

Why couldn't the Topeka music community come together annually to create inspirational music and to provide an opportunity for local players to get to enjoy one another's company, wondered the organizers. The experience had been too profound to let it end.

Danl Blackwood, Marta Barron and Ric Barron are old friends who have played in a number of bands and venues together. *Courtesy Marta Barron.*

The sound man rules! Sonny Heller gives directions to Danl Blackwood and Wyndi Senogles during the Jam4Dan. *Doug Ruth.*

When planning started for Jam4Dan II, it was decided scholarships would be the best way to memorialize Dan's immense influence on hundreds of guitar students over four decades. The event gained significant steam when local luthier Joel Edison donated a custom-built guitar that was raffled, with all proceeds going to the scholarship funds.

Starting with Jam4Dan II, Joel has contributed six guitars and counting. Dozens of bands have offered their talents at no charge with hundreds and hundreds of fans supporting the fundraiser. By 2010, so many high-quality bands wanted to participate, the event expanded to two days. In 2011, youth bands were added, which really reinforced the connection to the scholarship program. The youth portion was expanded in 2012. In 2013, a third night of entertainment was added. The Jam4Dan trustees are Mike Fox, Joel Edison, Tom Krebs, Danl Blackwood, J.D. Bloomar, Chris Aytes and Ed Carmona.

Scholarship applications contain three parts: a statement of need, the student's reflection on what his or her instrument/instruction means to him or her and a teacher recommendation. One of the great things about the scholarship program is that it does not discriminate when it comes to teachers. Proficiency on an instrument is the primary concern, not affiliation with a school or professional organization. Thus, the Jam4Dan scholarships benefit not only the students but also working musicians.

"Jam4Dan, as it inches towards its tenth year, has brought three important things to Topeka," said trustee, Tom Krebs, in 2014. "First, it's great fun for music lovers. Staged in the middle of the longest, coldest month, J4D is a great reason to get out of the house and break the cabin fever malaise. People regularly comment on what a great crowd it attracts." Tom continued:

Second, it [has] become a values showcase for the musicians. They know to bring their A game. As a result, set after set is top-quality music, but every now and then, there's the breakout performance. It could be a Saturday youth performer, someone new to the show, or a veteran band that blows the roof off. Those are special moments! And third, Jam4Dan brings out the best of Topeka. Bands donate over thirty performances each show…and love doing it. The flip side is Topeka youth are given an opportunity to grow musically, which in itself is a great opportunity, but it also gives them an opportunity, if they are paying attention, to learn about doing for others.

"In the end, the scholarships awarded, over $15,000 to date, are an important part of Jam4Dan but not the only upside," he said. "Community

Left: Urban Safari with Zeke Low on drums and Tommy Mills performing at the Celtic Fox. The band has been performing since 1993. Zeke began playing professionally at rec centers and other small venues at the age of fourteen, and he recalls what a great training ground for young musicians they were. As a member of the group Avalanche, he shared the stage with Duke Ellington shortly before the legend's death. *Doug Ruth.*

Opposite: Musician and luthier Joel Edison has made and donated several guitars for the Jam4Dan benefit over the years. Money raised goes to music scholarships. *Teri O'Trimble.*

building, musical and otherwise, and paying good things forward complement the scholarships to make for a valuable community contribution."

The community touched by Dan Falley goes on and on. His friend Doug Ruth said that he began as Dan's customer but that Dan taught him the ins and outs of music and the business.

Doug blogged about his friend on his website, TopekaTonight.com:

> *I first met Dan back in the mid-90s when I purchased an amp from him for my son.*
>
> *Years went by until 2003. I got back into the music scene after retiring from a local company. I was involved with a bluegrass/70's acoustic group. I started arranging gigs for the group and happened to stop by Dan's guitar shop.*
>
> *Dan became my mentor of the music business. From his long and successful career in music, he filled me in on what to expect and what to aim for. I remembered some basic rules he set forth for organizing a band:*

1. No drugs.

2. Everyone was expected to be prepared for practice.

3. There was no excuse for not showing up for a gig except being laid up in a hospital.

4. You gave every gig the best you had.

5. You gave the audience what they came to hear.

6. Set a goal with a deadline and pursue that goal without excuses.

I never heard Dan say anything negative about others. He always expected and hoped for the best of others. Sometimes, I could tell he was disappointed but he never said anything negative. This impressed me.

You could tell Dan really enjoyed playing with his latest group: Fyrestorm. From the lighting to the sound equipment to the performance, Dan always presented a top notch professional act. I still remember him asking the audience, "Is everyone having fun yet?" You could tell he was.

Those of us who have been around the block a few times realize that there are few people we can look back to who compared to an individual like

Dan Falley. Someone you could always count on. Someone who expected the best of himself and of others. And yet at the same time, not judging others when their actions disappointed him.

I feel fortunate to have called Dan a friend.

Dan left an entire community that can say the same.

4

DOUG RUTH AND WHEATSTOCK

A 2012 issue of *seveneightfive* magazine featured an interview by Tom Wah with music promoter Doug Ruth. Tom compared Doug to the magazine's founder, Kerrice Mapes, who created *seveneightfive* to highlight the art, music, food and entertainment scene in Topeka. Doug had established TopekaTonight on the web as the go-to place for the latest on Topeka musicians and venues years before the magazine was conceived.

"There wasn't any current resource that identified the individuals and bands involved in the live music scene in Topeka," Doug told Tom. Doug combined his love of music with his photographic skills to create the website.

"You can see Doug's great photographic eye, which can be traced to his days serving in Vietnam where he was assigned to a photographic squadron," wrote Tom. "There are over 10,000 pictures that track the many iterations of bands and solo artists that have played Topeka the last decade."

The article continued:

> Doug had moved to Topeka from Lansing, Michigan, in 1968 when the
> Air Force assigned him to Forbes Air Field. Although he was involved in
> the music scene when he was younger, it wasn't until 2003 that he became
> involved in music again. "I was leaving for lunch from the company I was
> working for and crossed paths with another employee who had a guitar. I
> found out that he and two others jammed over lunch hour. They invited me
> to join them. One thing led to another, and soon I was booking our little

The Cows with Stuart Yoho, Kenny Smith, Jim Edmiston and Terry Proctor have enjoyed a solid fan base since they began the coffee shop circuit decades ago. Often, the fans bring cowbells. *Doug Ruth.*

group, *The Boiler Room Boys.* Then, I started going to the area jams. I met the performers and realized music, not accounting, was my calling."

Not only did Doug create *TopekaTonight,* he was an early Topeka pioneer in promoting musical events featuring local talent. Long before there was *Jam4Dan, Rock the Block, LoudsoftLoud* and the *Singer/ Songwriter Showcases,* Doug produced his first Wheatstock, held at the Gage Amphitheatre on August 16, 2003. "It was at this time in my life that I was able to retire after thirty years auditing hospitals. Wheatstock came about with the idea of celebrating the music attitude of Woodstock back in 1969."

After a move from Gage Park to the downtown Ramada, Wheatstock celebrated its third year in Old Prairie Town at Ward Meade Park…The music festival featured a number of hot new artists in town as well as established standouts.

"The individuals and bands that have been involved over the years are some of the best talent we have in the area," Doug says. "The music can be described as 'Americana.' Basically everything from folk to bluegrass, but mainly acoustic music.

Doug has shifted the focus somewhat and does not visit as many venues as he did in those early days. Tom noted that Doug's commitment to fitness and turning his life around (he lost eighty pounds in eight months several years ago) and his generosity in promoting other musicians are qualities to be admired and emulated.

When Doug approached me about my alter ego's (Dixie Lee Jackson) taking over the emcee duties at Wheatstock, Dixie and I were both thrilled. Dixie Lee was especially thrilled at sharing the Entertainer of the Year award with the Wood Valley Pickers in 2014. The Shyster Mountain Gang received the Lifetime Achievement Award.

The awards became a part of the event in 2006. Performers honored include Glenn Osborn, Teresa Cuevas, Andy McKee, Kerry Livgren, Greg Fox, Kenny Smith and Bridges, Gary Bisel, Randy Wills, Judy Coder and Pride of the Prairie and Dan Falley.

Doug recalled how Dan Falley had helped him in the early years of Wheatstock.

"Dan helped me with the lighting for Wheatstock III, August 2006," recalled Doug. "He came by on Friday night to set up the lighting at the Ramada Downtown ballroom. The next day, he spent the whole day ensuring the lighting was proper. He was a great help, along with Dan Kaufman of Steam Music, who was handling the sound. In my opinion, they are two of the top professionals in Topeka. The two Dans, along with the performers, made Wheatstock III a success."

"I can recall many times when I'd get impatient with certain developments concerning putting on various music shows," Doug added. "Dan would sit me down and tell me the reality of the music industry. I really appreciated his advice."

For those involved in staging the event, specifically Doug, Old Prairie Town director John Bell and the Shawnee County Parks and Rec staff, it is a very long day and a busy week leading up to it.

"Wheatstock is special because we're showcasing some of the best local musicians in Shawnee County," said John. "We have tremendous talent here in Shawnee County, and we try to showcase that during Wheatstock. The bands donate their time, quite enthusiastically, and that is pretty much because of Doug. His generosity in promoting musicians and venues is appreciated and returned."

The setting, Old Prairie Town at Ward-Meade Park, is so appropriate. The site of one of the pioneering families of Kansas along the Oregon Trail, there is a reconstruction of their original cabin, and the subsequent mansion

The Solohogs have reunited after a long hiatus with (left to right) Les Goering, Mike Stratton and Lew Spring. *Doug Ruth*.

is a museum and park offices. The gardens are a tourist attraction year round. A school, church, general store and other buildings have been added over the years and reinforce the feeling of a small town. If there could be a collective homecoming for all of Kansas, this is the place it should be. From the beginning, this has been a family-friendly event, and as the children frolic in the grass or folks enjoy a Green River soda from the Potwin Drug Store, it is quite evident that there is no place like home.

5
WALNUT VALLEY FESTIVAL

I lived in Kansas for nearly two decades before I went to Winfield. There are few things I am more ashamed to admit. There were lots of reasons: time, money, partners. But underlying it all was basic snobbery. It began in Fancy Gap, Virginia, when my sister and I were putting out that magazine, *A Comin' and A Goin'*. We published festival schedules from all over but mostly from the southeast. Then we got on the Walnut Valley mailing list. I distinctly remember opening that flyer and thinking, Kansas! What do they know about bluegrass in Kansas? After all, *we* invented it—I try not to think of all the years I wasted because of my foolish pride.

The Walnut Valley Association was formed in 1972, with "its sole purpose to produce the Walnut Valley National Guitar Flat-Picking Championships Festival," said organizers. The event has evolved from two days in 1972 to the current four-day festival every third weekend of September. Entertainment is offered on four stages simultaneously. In addition, there is a juried arts and crafts fair, workshops and acoustic instrument contests.

"What began with ten acts and two contests now boasts over forty acts and eight contests," said organizers, "including one international contest, five national contests and two Walnut Valley contests."

Competition is a big part of the festival's having attracted more than three thousand contestants from the United States and other countries. Australia, Canada, Denmark, Sweden, England, Germany, Italy, Japan, New Caledonia, Switzerland and Wales are some of the countries and territories that have been represented.

The contests are the National Flat Pick Championships and the National Finger Pick Championships. Additionally, the Walnut Valley Festival hosts the International Autoharp, National Mountain Dulcimer, National Hammered Dulcimer, National Bluegrass Banjo, Walnut Valley Old Time Fiddle and Walnut Valley Mandolin Championships.

"Well-known Winfield winners include Mark O'Connor of Nashville, Tennessee, who has won or placed in more Walnut Valley Festival contests than any other contestant. Mark won the National Guitar Flat-Picking Championship in 1975 and 1977," said officials, "and also won the Walnut Valley Fiddle Championship in 1974 and 1977. Alison Krauss of Nashville won the Walnut Valley Fiddle Championship in 1984 and Steve Kaufman of Alcoa, Tennessee, is the only three-time winner of the National Guitar Flat-Picking Contest, having won in the years 1978, 1984, and 1986 respectively. (Tennessee has consistently produced the most winners over the years.) Other Winfield winners include Mandolin virtuoso Chris Thile, the Mandolin Champion in 1993 and Dixie Chick fiddler Martie Erwin Seidel in 1987 and '89."

Nearly fifteen thousand people attend as spectators, but many of those come fully loaded with instrument cases slung over their backs. The pros who appear onstage often meander through the campsites themselves, stopping to pick one with attendees.

"In 1991, our twentieth anniversary year, an attempt was made to host the world's largest acoustic string band," an official said. "When the time came, 770 musicians held their instruments skyward and played 'Will the Circle Be Unbroken.'"

The family-friendly event has hosted many private gatherings, including reunions and weddings. In 2011, Mike and Libby Adams tied the knot on Stage 2. They were going to be in Winfield anyway.

"We were wanting a date in September, and since we were going to be in Winfield for the festival, as well as quite a few of our friends, we decided it was the perfect place," said Libby.

"Well, we were going to get married at Stage Five. But it had poured rain most of the morning, so we asked the T-shirt guy if we could get married in the breeze way by Stage Two. Right before it was time for our ceremony, the clouds broke and the sun came through, so we got married at Stage Two while they were resetting the equipment after the rain."

The festival is far more than bluegrass. It now is a blend of all kinds of acoustic music: bluegrass, folk, old-time country, a little bit cowboy, some Irish, blues, Cajun and more. And the bluegrass is both traditional and progressive.

Among those who have appeared on stage at the Walnut Valley Festival are Lester Flatt, Doc & Merle Watson, Mark O'Connor, Alison Krauss, Mike Snider, Byron Berline, Dan Crary, Norman Blake, John Hartford, Tom Chapin, David Grisman, Merle Travis, Mike Cross, New Grass Revival, Hot Rize, Nickel Creek, David Holt, DeDannan (Irish), Tony Rice, Jim & Jesse, Jimmy Driftwood, Don Reno, Buck White, Red Clay Ramblers, Gamble Rogers, Joel Mabus, Bryan Bowers, Front Porch String Band, Robin & Linda Williams, the Dixie Chicks, Doug Dillard, Tom Paxton, John McCutcheon and many more.

In 1999, the International Bluegrass Music Association (IBMA) selected the Walnut Valley Festival to receive the first ever "IBMA Bluegrass Event of the Year."

"Most of all, the festival is a homecoming," said one official, "and a homecoming not just because of the music and how folks act, but a coming home to a place in the soul and the heart with a spirit of celebration."

My friends who have been attending Winfield for decades have entrenched traditions and established camp spots. The legendary "land rush" for campsites each year would put the "Sooners" to shame. Luxurious motor homes and modest tents squeeze together around the campfire where music is made each night until the wee hours. The "Fugarwes" and the "Bucket Camp" set up side by side each year in their little corner of the Cowley County Fairgrounds with folks from different parts of Kansas and Nebraska greeting one another with hugs and howdies like a family reunion.

The Walnut Valley Festival, like all successful events, occurs in many places, on many levels, in many ways. The good folks from Nebraska treat the Bucket Camp to Café Luigi each year and prepare a meal of spaghetti and wine, serving fellow campers and treating them like honored guests. The tables and campsite are decorated like a quaint bistro, the food is wonderful and there is, of course, music. Afterward, all gather around the fire and join together in singing "Will the Circle Be Unbroken." Those friends since gone are remembered; those friends still here are cherished. There is much laughter and a few tears.

One of those whose memory is cherished is Shirley Renner. "Aunt Shirley" succumbed to breast cancer on January 17, 2013. Her daughter, Penny Clabaugh, described her mom's feeling for Winfield.

"Winfield had a special place in Mom's heart," said Penny. "I'm not sure which part of Winfield got her hooked, the thrill of land rush, the music, the camping with friends and family, playing by the camp fires or the flea market shopping halls. We can't forget the Winfield garage sales—all of

Sue Ann Seel (far left), winner of a children's songwriting competition at the Walnut Valley Festival, with her co-writers and performers, Dianna Burrup (center) and Amy Nixon (right). *Rod Seel.*

which she loved. Her heart and soul were in the whole Winfield experience, and everyone around her was infected by the joy she experienced while she was there."

Her nephew, Dave Houser, remarked of her passing, "Someone once said 'No man is an island.' I believe that's so in the sense that we are all made up of not only our genetic building blocks but are formed and melded by those we meet and interact with throughout our lives, some more than others."

"Uncle Bill and Aunt Shirley were a huge part of my and Kim's lives as well as everyone that ever met them. We lost half of that Dynamic Duo…Shirley will always be with us, in our hearts and thoughts for as long as we continue to live and play and love."

Shirley's final days were spent surrounded by the friends and family who loved her. Playing in the background were the tapes recorded around those firesides at Winfield. Nothing more meaningful can be said about an event that has come to be a part of so many lives.

This is an event that my friend Sue Ann Seel and I share a passion for. She shared her reflections on attending the festival for the first time:

> *I am new to this whole thing. At forty-six years old, because it was always something I wanted to do, I bought a banjo. Don't ask why, because I don't know; it's just something I always wanted to do. And so last August, I bought myself a banjo. Being innocent of the disdain many guitar players have of my chosen vice, I set out to find a teacher. It took me a while, and I received some rejection from the guitar players I asked, but finally, I found a banjo teacher—and I found a good one! That was so much fun I bought a guitar and began to learn it, too. I even joined the Kansas Bluegrasss Association! But the strangest thing kept happening. My teacher kept asking me if I was going to Winfield. Every time I went to the music store to buy strings or just drool over other instruments, someone would ask me, "Are you going to Winfield?" I should have known then that something was up.*
>
> *Of course I had heard of Winfield. I knew it was a town in Kansas. I also knew they had a music festival "down there" every fall. But there my knowledge stopped. And so when I decided to go this year, if [only] for a little while, I should have known something was up from the glee on my banjo teacher's face.*
>
> *I also should have known something was up when we pulled into line to buy tickets on the big day. The very fun woman who helped us said, "You only buying a day pass? It won't be enough." Oh, man, was she right! I was hooked from the minute I walked into the fairgrounds. The food (I still*

have funnel cake sugar on my banjo case) was enough to pull me in. But the music. It was everywhere. How do you decide which stage to go to when everywhere you turn the most wonderful music [is] pouring forth? Talk about babes in candy stores! I was driving my poor husband nuts because I couldn't decide which direction to turn first! And I loved watching the competitions. I was soaking things up like a sponge. Of course I had fun in the arts and crafts buildings. And when I went into the building where the musical vendors were, my husband stopped me and made me hand over the credit card. When he found me eyeing a banjo that was several times my monthly salary, I am sure he was glad he had wrestled my ability to pay for it away from me!

But the more I listened and the more I watched, the more my fingers were itching to get on a fret board. Fortunately for this rookie, my teacher was there, and so I made the trek back to the car to get the banjo and headed off for the campsite where my teacher was staying. I was very nervous about jamming with musicians so much better than me, about violating some unwritten rule about who could play where and when, inner and outer circles and all, and I was embarrassed about my rookie status. But when I got to the campsite and opened up my case, all was forgotten. It was early evening when I got there, and when seemingly a few minutes of musical bliss had passed and I looked at my watch, it was 11:00 p.m. Soon I would need to pack up and leave, for the lady at the gate had warned me that we would turn into banjo-toting pumpkins if we didn't leave by midnight. I left with great regret, knowing full well had I stayed I would have played all night.

I am hooked.

How many days to Winfield?

I have been fortunate to experience Winfield not only as a spectator, wandering from site to site with music and wood smoke in the air, but also from behind the scenes as a member of the press. People can be very different backstage or "off the record"—not so at Winfield.

When I sat down with Kansas native son Dan Crary, master of the guitar, I was more than a little awed. Not only is he truly a musical legend, but he is also bright and articulate—a master of language. He is not what outsiders expect at a bluegrass festival. I had grown up listening to this Kansan perform with Berline, Crary and Hickman and California. He had seemed foreign to me back then, such a virtuoso, such perfection in his performances. I expected him to be distant and arrogant. Nothing could have been further

Dan Crary, a true virtuoso of the guitar, is originally from Kansas City and attended the University of Kansas. *Courtesy Dan Crary.*

from the truth. He is a gentleman with an artist's sensibilities and a very real commitment to excellence. Dan freely talked of growing up in Kansas City and his early musical influences, Elvis for one. "For the first time," recalled Dan, "there was a guitar player up front!"

Troll Hollow

Sue Ann Seel

There is a mystical magical musical place called Troll Hollow. Once every year, this very special place rises up out of the mists of the Walnut River and nestles itself into a quiet, tree-filled spot in the valley underneath the great Walnut River bridge. The inhabitants of Troll Hollow, who appear there once a year as well, are a jolly folk, known for their music and merrymaking. As the folk begin to arrive, their little homes pop up like mushrooms after a rain in the valley. Some of the homes are brightly colored cloth domes; others are box-shaped huts with wheels. As the homes pop up, the people make camp, and then they commence to make music, each with the kind of music that is unique to him or her. The folk have special instruments, most stringed, and the music they make is unrivaled anywhere in the day-to-day world. And my, but they can play, and they play all the time, when they are not eating from the little booths that spring up on the main street or dancing in the grove, where roaming bands of traveling troubadours perform for the revelers. The folk who live in Troll Hollow are kindred musical spirits, and they try to truly live in peace and harmony with one another. Troll Hollow is a happy place, where folks can go to escape the blues—or play them, if they prefer! Sadly, Troll Hollow lives in our world only for five days a year, in the fall, when the temperatures are cool and crisp and the leaves are just beginning to be tipped in color. But never fear, dear readers. For while Troll Hollow only exists in this world for five melodious days of the year, it can live forever in our hearts, if only we will let it.

Dan performs as a solo artist and with his band Thunderation, featuring veteran musician and prolific songwriter Steve Spurgin on bass and Martin Stevens on mandolin. The music produced by these three will cause you to rethink instruments and just what they are capable of. Steve said that he found "playing music with Dan Crary a bit distracting."

"I keep listening to what he's up to and forget where I am myself," he said. "I have to stop being a fan and concentrate."

Dan also partners with Beppe Gambetta, who hails from Genova, and is widely recognized as one of Europe's leading guitarists. When these two take the stage, well, it would take a symphony to produce a bigger sound.

With dozens of comparable headliners, the Walnut Valley Festival ensures that crowd favorites will take one of the several stages throughout the event. (You haven't lived until you have heard Winfield favorites Mountain Smoke perform "Armadillo Suicide" or John Hartford's "Tall Buildings.") It's no wonder that Sue Ann and I are not the only ones counting down the days. My favorite bluegrass and old-time shows, *Trail Mix* on Kansas Public Radio and *Farmer's Turnpike* on 92.9 the Bull hype, the performers with personal participation. There are friends who ease into and out of the Winfield season with pre-Winfield and post-Winfield parties. Vacation plans are made to coincide with the festival schedule. Money is laid aside; campers and gear are cleaned and packed. New strings are purchased. Throughout Kansas and far beyond, people are asking, "How many days until Winfield?"

6

MARIACHI ESTRELLA DE TOPEKA

By Lisa Sandmeyer

Though one night of horror brought an end to the groundbreaking group Mariachi Estrella de Topeka, the legacy left by seven Topeka women lives on.

The first all-female mariachi band in Kansas—one of the first in the United States—was taking its show on the road to a corporate event in Kansas City, Missouri. The women were on their way to change for the performance, cutting across the lobby of the Hyatt Regency Hotel on its skywalks, when the walkway collapsed. Four members of the band were among the 114 people who died that night, July 17, 1981.

Connie Alcala, Dolores Carmona, Teresa Cuevas, Dolores Galván, Isabel González, Rachel Galván Sangalang and Linda Scurlock started their musical journey together at Our Lady of Guadalupe Church in the Oakland neighborhood of Topeka. The church is the sponsor of Fiesta Mexicana, a weeklong fundraiser that has been a mainstay of summers in the capital city since 1933.

They first performed in church, and as they spent more time together, they moved toward the lively music of the mariachi band. Linda Scurlock was not a parishioner at the church, but she brought her trumpet to the band, adding to the signature sound. Their talents continued to grow.

Mariachi Estrella de Topeka was on the verge of a record deal when the sky fell in. The Hyatt collapse claimed the lives of Connie Alcala, Dolores Carmona, Dolores Galván and Linda Sculock. Isabel González had stayed home that night for her children. Teresa Cuevas recounted that night many

Traditional Mexican music means traditional Mexican dancing. The sounds and colors are a feast for the senses. Louise Pedrosa paints with traditional materials in the gouache method. *Louise Neal Pedrosa.*

times, telling how she called for help from under a pile of concrete and heard a voice yelling, "There's a live one!"

Cuevas was alive indeed, and for the next thirty years, she mentored female mariachi musicians, obtaining further training in the genre herself.

The memorial to members of Mariachi de Estrella Topeka, who died in the collapse of the Hyatt Regency in Kansas City. The statue is on the grounds of the Topeka Performing Arts Center. *Noel Coalson.*

Another half dozen mariachi bands with female members in Topeka can trace their beginnings to Cuevas and Mariachi Estrella.

On the twenty-fifth anniversary of the Hyatt skywalk's collapse, a statue honoring the four members of Mariachi Estrella de Topeka who died there was unveiled on the grounds of the Topeka Performing Arts Center. Called *Mariachi Divina*, it depicts a woman reaching heavenward to the stars—*las estrellas*.

7

THE BAND KANSAS

Sound checks for the night's performance were underway at Liberty Hall in Lawrence. The musicians who were being honored by the Kansas Music Hall of Fame seemed far more intent on greeting old friends than hurrying to the stage. Greg Allen, architect and supporter of many of the same historic projects as I, was in the foyer, and I paused to chat. Phil Ehart, drummer and founding member of the band Kansas, walked up and looked at us quizzically.

"You two know each other?" he asked.

"Yes, I've known Greg for years. We've served on committees together."

"Greg serves on committees?" Phil responded. "What does he do on these committees?"

"Well, he mostly tells us why we can't do things when we have big ideas," I said.

Phil nodded and walked away. I didn't even ask Greg why he was there during sound check. I knew he had grown up with several of the inductees. I went into the theater just as Greg was taking center stage with the band, White Clover. As he stepped up to the microphone, he was transformed from mild-mannered architect to rock star. Belting out the Allman Brothers tune "Statesboro Blues," Greg revived the vocals that had characterized the band more than thirty years earlier.

I scrambled to get his autograph.

The group White Clover later evolved into Kansas, and several musicians performed with both groups. Greg, who works with Schwerdt Design Group in Topeka, left the band to return to architecture school. Looking back, he said he believes it was the right move for him.

White Clover, the band that evolved into Kansas, being inducted into the KMHOF. Members are (left to right) Warren Eisenstein, Jeff Glixman, Greg Hartline, Rich Williams, Greg Allen and Bill Fast, and Phil Ehart is at the podium. *Deb Bisel.*

Former band mate Richard Williams, still a member of Kansas, compared making music to breathing and knows that for him, music was a calling. This was his third induction into the hall of fame (the first two were with Kansas and Plain Jane) but the first he has been able to attend due to the band's touring schedule. Williams has lived in Atlanta since the mid-1970s.

Williams and current band mate drummer Phil Ehart joined several of the former band members on stage. Bill Fast recalled that Phil actually hired him for a group called the Sheffields, a dance band:

> *Even after we became White Clover, Greg Allen and I would have the occasional Sam & Dave moment, and it was a blast! To this day the R&B sound is my favorite, and it was very much a part of the music scene in Kansas during the '60s and '70s.*
>
> *I had lusted after the cool curves of an electric guitar before the "British Invasion" came along, but that Sunday night on* Ed Sullivan, *the Beatles hooked me, too. Having spent many a night listing to KOMA, WLS and KAAY, I was already a big fan of the R&B acts like the Isley Brothers, Bo Diddly*

*and James Brown. There were also older guys I knew who dug the R&B stuff
and were in bands or putting something together. A band that deserves way more
credit from back then was the Group. Lane Tietgen and the guys were good solid
musicians with a funky sound. We used to sneak out at night in junior high to
see Finnigan and the SERFS at the Touch-of-Gold club (had to stand outside
in the parking lot and look through the big ventillation fans!).*

*So even though my first real band, the Vegetables (Sam Crow, Forrest
Chapman, Tim Carkhuff and I), played Yardbirds, BGs and Animals
tunes, I was still out there wanting to play "dance" music.*

Among them was former Topekan Dave Hope, who left the band Kansas
in the 1980s and became an Anglican priest. His Florida congregation
wasn't thrilled, he quipped, that he was leaving his pastoral duties to accept
an award for being a rock 'n' roll musician. Dave's comment was tongue-in-
cheek. His congregation was, in fact, very excited for him.

"I told them I'm still a band guy at heart," said Hope, adding that his
band mates are never far from his mind.

As he was performing Ash Wednesday services, placing the ashes on his
congregants' foreheads and repeating the words, "From dust thou came, to
dust thou shalt return," he had Kerry Livgren's song "Dust in the Wind"
running through his mind, and he had to stifle a chuckle. The reunion with
his friends was meaningful beyond words, he said: "These people are not just
my family—they are the fabric of my life."

Rick Roberts, musician and owner of Kansas Guitar, recalls his being a
White Clover fan.

"When I was a kid, there were bands everywhere. Great bands. On Friday
nights, I'd go to the Crestview Rec Center and hear local bands," he said. "The
Pets, the Gimlets, the Thingies. I'd stand in front of the speakers and soak it all in.
It was an awesome time. Many of those players went on to the big time. We've
lost a few, like Warren Eisenstein, who was in the Cocky Fox and White Clover."

"Warren was the best around. He, they, meaning White Clover, would
open for national acts and he WAS the show," said Rick. "I have two pics
of him after he knew he had cancer. What did he do? He drove a NASCAR
at 150 miles per hour! Warren was from Brooklyn, New York. He came
to Kansas to go to Kansas University. Growing up in New York, the local
players would play The Catskills in the summertime. He knew Leslie West
(Westheimer) of the band Mountain. He knew Billy Joel."

Warren's death in early 2014 was a tremendous loss to the musical
community. His obituary read, in part, "He will always be remembered by

Warren Eisenstein performs with the band White Clover at its KMHOF induction. *Beth Meyers.*

his friends as one of the most creative and funniest people ever. His wit and ability to mimic anyone was amazing. He could also play a guitar and sing like few others could. On most weekends, he could be found jamming in Dallas area clubs until his illness prevented him from doing so." The obituary went on to include "current and former members of the band Kansas" as the loved ones and friends who survived him.

Celebrating its fortieth year as a band in 2013, Kansas's first public statement appeared on its self-titled album in 1974. "From the beginning, we considered ourselves and our music different and we hope we will always remain so."

Little did this legendary rock group realize that back in the early '70s, what seemed to be "different" was actually ahead of its time. This garage band from Topeka was discovered by Wally Gold, who worked for Don Kirshner, and released its first album in 1974.

Gold's son, Eric, remembers that magic moment when his dad discovered Kansas.

"From the moment Dad first brought the Kansas demo tape home, sat down in the 'music room' with me, and played 'Can I Tell You' at high volume," said Eric, "there was a distinct gleam in his eyes. In his role as VP/general manager at Don Kirshner Music, his job was to find new talent. He knew at that moment he had greatly exceeded Donny's expectations. He had found something very special."

"Dad completely loved the music. Sure he discovered and produced them, but he was also one of the biggest Kansas fans you'll ever find. And he became very close with the guys—relationships that lasted long after he stopped working closely with the band. Of all of Dad's accomplishments in the music business (and there were many)," Eric continued, "I believe that he felt that his work with Kansas was his 'crown jewel.' He was so proud that he could find this amazing collection of talent and bring their magic to the world. And he made some close friends in the process."

The band has produced eight gold albums, three sextuple-platinum albums (*Leftoverture*, *Point of Know Return*, *Best of Kansas*), one platinum live album (*Two for the Show*) and a million-selling gold single, "Dust in the Wind." Kansas appeared on the *Billboard* charts for over two hundred weeks throughout the '70s and '80s and played to sold-out arenas and stadiums throughout North America, Europe and Japan. In fact, "Carry On Wayward Son" was the number-two most played track on classic rock radio in 1995 and went to number one in 1997.

In 1998, Kansas released an orchestral album, *Always Never the Same*, recorded with the London Symphony Orchestra at Abbey Road Studios. The band followed with an orchestral tour accompanied by top-caliber symphony orchestras. In 2000, Kansas went back into the studio with original band member and songwriter Kerry Livgren to produce *Somewhere to Elsewhere*, the first album featuring all six of the original players in twenty years. The ten new songs were written by Kerry Livgren and recorded in his studio in Topeka, Kansas. Players included Phil Ehart, Billy Greer, Dave

During sound checks at Liberty Hall for the KMHOF induction, members of White Clover rehearse: (left to right) Richard Williams, Jeff Glixman and David Hope. *Beth Meyers.*

Hope, Kerry Livgren, Robby Steinhardt, Steve Walsh and Richard Williams.

In 2009, in their hometown of Topeka, Kansas's members celebrated their thirty-fifth anniversary with a symphonic concert, accompanied by the Washburn University Symphony Orchestra, conducted by Larry Baird. The DVD release *There's Know Place Like Home* captured this unique live performance and featured special guests Kerry Livgren and Steve Morse.

In 2013, their hometown welcomed them once again as they were inducted into the Kansas Hall of Fame. Other honorees were Clark Kent/Superman, James Naismith, the Menninger family and the First Kansas Colored Volunteer Infantry. Rich Williams commented that one of the reasons the band members had stayed together all these years was the value system they grew up with. "I had a Beaver Cleaver upbringing," he said. "Very normal, very blue collar."

He still considers himself blue collar. "I'm just a guy who plays guitar."

Kerry spoke for the band at the award ceremony and said he had not realized how emotional this would be for him. Later, when asked about being inducted into the Rock 'n' roll Hall of Fame, he said it meant much more to be honored by his home state.

The band Kansas was inducted into the Kansas Hall of Fame during its fortieth anniversary year, 2013. *From left to right*: presenter Christyna Luna, emcee Barry Feaker, Jeff Glixman, Phil Ehart, Robby Steinhardt, David Ragsdale, presenter Suzie Gilbert, Billy Greer, Richard Williams and Kerry Livgren. Lead singer Steve Walsh was ill and unable to attend, and the original bassist, Dave Hope, was also unavailable. *Danl Blackwood.*

The band, while evolving, has managed to maintain its distinctive sound, perhaps because new members loved that sound so much. David Ragsdale was already a fan before he joined Kansas.

"I was riding down the road with the radio on, and a song came on, 'Can I Tell You'—there was a violin. I thought, Oh my goodness!" His mom had pushed him toward violin, but he wanted the cooler guitar instead. But hearing Kansas made him realize violin could have a place in rock music. David would join the group when founding member Robby Steinhardt left.

Likewise, Billy Greer was playing in bands throughout the Southeast, covering Kansas songs. "I probably played some of these songs more than the guys in the band," he said. "We'd play a set in some club and play 'Carry On My Wayward Son' twice in one night."

Vocalist/keyboardist Steve Walsh left in 2014, after forty-one years. The news sent a shock wave through loyal fans.

"[I] hope that Steve Walsh is enjoying the decompression of being the lead singer for Kansas after all these years," said Randy Johnson. "[We] will miss his stage presence and energy, but [we] know that he has reached the point to enjoy the fruits of his labors and look back with pride of a job well done. His voice and the music of Kansas will live on forever."

The new lead vocalist is Ronnie Platt, formerly of Shooting Star.

"I want Kansas fans to know, first and foremost, I'm one of them," says Platt in a statement on the band's Facebook page. "I'm a long-time [*sic*] fan of the music and have always looked up to Steve Walsh. My goal is not to replace Steve; no one can do that. It is my goal and responsibility to sustain the integrity that is Kansas. This is a lifelong dream and I would like to thank Phil, Rich, Billy, and David for the opportunity. Yes, I've got the job, but now it's time to earn it…and I take nothing for granted that has been given to me. My performance in Kansas will be how I've always performed, with passion and enthusiasm."

"After considering other candidates, it became clear Ronnie was our guy," Phil Ehart said. "He's a perfect fit musically and personally with the band. His passion for the band and the music, as well as his musicianship, is exceptional."

Of course it is. Anything less, and it wouldn't be Kansas.

The loyal legion of Kansas fans call themselves "Wheatheads." Rarely has a band enjoyed such a faithful and thoroughly grounded following. Most have been fans for decades. Many have attended dozens of concerts in those years. What inspires such loyalty?

"Kansas has introduced me to a whole new genre of music," answered Eugene "Danger" Schreder. "Their contributions to progressive rock have been more than influential, as well as their influence on my life. Kansas is a state of mind."

Lisa Larue Baker

As a small girl, my grandmother played music all of the time around the house. She would play movie soundtracks, and *Camelot* was one of the biggest influences on me, ever. She knew all of the DJs on KTOP and WREN, and they would give us promotional copies of records that I would play along with on my little Magnus Chord Organ. Later, I graduated to a Hammond organ from

Theo Landon played not only the piano but also the harp. As the first lady of Kansas, her musical ability was widely known and enjoyed. Hiding behind the harp is the future U.S. senator Nancy Landon Kassebaum Baker, and her younger brother, John, is in the foreground. *Sarah McNeive Research Room, Historic Topeka Cemetery.*

Jenkins Music store and would sometimes play for shoppers on the mezzanine at Pelletiers (department store) and also at Montgomery Ward.

I didn't have much experience on the piano, except for playing the beautiful grand piano at Alf Landon's house. My grandfather would take me with him when he'd go visit on Friday nights, and Mrs. Landon would let me play.

But when I saw Steve Walsh from Kansas doing these incredible things on an organ much like the one in our living room, I knew *that* was what I wanted to do. And if these guys from Topeka, just like me, could do it, well, so could I. Then I saw the other Topeka band with two keyboardists—Alchemy, with Mike Kelso and Joe Green. I was determined.

Today, I am a progressive rock keyboardist with eight albums and have worked with folks such as John Payne from the band Asia, Michael Sadler from the supergroup Saga and many others. My band has even been nominated as instrumental band of the year at the Hollywood Music Awards. I hope that I can be an inspiration for some other little Topeka girl who will say, "If that girl from Topeka can reach her dreams, so can I!"

8

STAGE AND SCREEN

Much of the music and many of the lyrics that we hum or sing comes from the soundtrack of a movie or from the stage. That music takes on a life of its own beyond its role in furthering the dramatic action. It becomes a part of us in profound and intimate ways.

When Shannon Reilly marked his twenty-second year with Topeka Civic Theatre and Academy, he did so by tackling the most ambitious of musicals—*Les Miserable*. Challenging for any theater group, it is especially so for a group of volunteers. The result was astounding and secured Shannon's reputation for choosing and encouraging amazing talent.

Founded in 1936, TCTA is the oldest continuously running community dinner theater in the country. The quality of TCTA's productions has remained consistent through throughout the decades. I simply cannot give them a bad review.

In July 1999, TCTA completed construction of its new home in the former Gage Elementary School. The school was built around 1929 and is rich in architecture and design. It also affords two stages, the main stage for the larger productions and the Oldfather's Theatre, which is a more intimate setting. In 2013, TCTA began a partnership with Shawnee County to manage Helen Hocker Theater in Gage Park. Through that partnership, TCTA continues to enrich theater programming at HHT and through outreach programs throughout Shawnee County. Residents of northeast Kansas flock to fill the seats no matter which stage is being used.

The theater has achieved much recognition since finding a permanent home where its creative energies could at last be focused on production values. In 1975, managing director Don Bachmann's production of *One Flew Over the Cuckoo's Nest* won the state community theater festival and advanced to the regional in Omaha. In 1979, Bachmann's production of *The Good Doctor*, starring Charley Oldfather, went all the way to nationals, won it and represented the United States at an international amateur theater festival the following spring in Dundalk, Ireland.

In 1981, P.K. Worley's production of *Jacques Brel Is Alive and Well and Living in Paris* won the state festival and was performed at the regional in Topeka. Terrance McKerrs took two productions to nationals in 1985, *I'm Getting My Act Together* and *Taking It on the Road*, which won third place, and he won again for *The Taffetas* in 1991, which won second place while McKerrs won the Best Director award.

Speaking of directors, Ken Spurgeon was a mild-mannered schoolteacher in Andover when he conceived the notion that he would make documentaries about the Kansas history he loves so much. He founded Lone Chimney Films with friend Jon Goering in 2003. The company completed its first documentary, *Touched by Fire: Bleeding Kansas, 1854–1861*, in the spring of 2005. In 2006, LCF was granted status as a not-for-profit organization and began preproduction work on its second documentary, *Bloody Dawn: The Lawrence Massacre*. That film was completed in late 2007, and both films have aired over twenty times on PBS regional stations across Kansas, Missouri, Oklahoma, Iowa and Nebraska. Both films have also been used in more than two hundred classrooms.

In late 2013, LCF released *The Road to Valhalla*, which details the story of the Kansas-Missouri border war (1861–65) and the legacy of the war, especially in Kansas. LCF is also in the script and preproduction phase on a documentary about Kansas's early aviation, *Borne on the South Wind*, in addition to films about the Kansas-Oklahoma Land Run and Kansas's role in the Great Depression. *The Road to Valhalla* has been shown in theaters around Kansas and in New York and New Jersey and will be aired on television as well.

Ken was so careful about the script, the actors, the historians, the set, the props—all the details integral to a quality production. But experience and his own artistic sensibilities had taught him that equally important, even in a documentary, is music:

> *Music moves and inspires. I think in more ways than one, music can be transcendent. In the case of music from our past, it has the ability to connect*

us with those who went before, and in that way, we remain connected. When we chose music for any of our films, it was a fun but difficult process to try to have the music match the feeling created visually.

Looking back at our projects now, I realize that in each film, we had diverse elements. Jon Goering and the Free Staters were the essential drivers in our first film, Touched by Fire: Bleeding Kansas, *but Jon and I both searched for other sounds as well. In our second film,* Bloody Dawn: The Lawrence Massacre, *we began to utilize not only the talent but also the songwriting talents of Jed Marum, an American folk musician. Finally, with our most recent film,* The Road to Valhalla, *it was a tremendous joy to be able to work with Jed in more of a composer's role.*

Since the project was in development for almost five years, Jed and I had the opportunity to talk about the film both in a larger sense and in a specific sense. Jed's love of history and understanding of so many historical melodies was a great asset. Still, it was his songwriting that I wanted to tap into further and that I feel really elevated the feel of the film. Again, we had the opportunity to use other musicians in various studio tracks, most notably, through the advice and consultation of the talented Orin Friesen, we were able to add Michael Martin Murphey's wonderful talents to the film and soundtrack. Michael, like Jed, has the passion not just for the music but also for the history that is essential to such a project. Rather than simply playing the music, both men feel a responsibility to get it right, both in the musical sense and in the historical sense.

The Road to Valhalla *is the story of the Kansas-Missouri border before and during the Civil War. So often we can all get lost in the politics, the battles and the details. But what we often forget is the thousands of people caught in the middle of the conflict. For those who were players in that dangerous and deadly drama, the war was the defining event of their lives and whether they died during the war or many years later, they were all on the shared Road to Valhalla.*

The music Ken chose achieved all he envisioned, and his films would not be as effective without these melodies and lyrics. The viewer may forget what the history lesson was supposed to be, but he or she will not forget how the songs made them feel and how they communicated the experience. Jed's originals, "Even as I Ramble," which reduces Ken to tears, and "Shines Like Gold," which reduces me to tears, have the feel of classics. Ken said that the former is his favorite of Jed's compositions for LCF "because of…how it captures the idea of our lives and the unknown twists and turns." Both songs

Michael Martin Murphey appeared in the film *The Road to Valhalla*, where he sings "Lorena," a campfire favorite for soldiers on both sides of America's Civil War. *Courtesy Lone Chimney Films.*

touch on the idea of the battles and hardships along the road and the joyous reunion in Valhalla. Other originals for LCF projects that were inspired by events in Kansas history include "Lone Chimney," a graphic monument to the destruction of homes and farms along the border, and "One Bloody Friday," about William Clarke Quantrill's 1863 raid on Lawrence. The film crew chose to reinterpret some standards from those days, and Michael Martin Murphey's renditions of "Lorena" and "The Girl I Left Behind Me" are simple, expressive and profound. As soon as the Kansas Territory had forts, it had men leaving them and the regimental bands struck up the classic farewell song. These recordings truly bring that era of American history to life in a way that words, and even the landscape itself, cannot. Likewise, the classic "Battle Cry of Freedom" gets a historically accurate treatment with brass instruments, reflective of the military bands of the era.

9

LITTLE HOUSE
ON THE PRAIRIE

O ne of America's most cherished and beloved stories is the Little House series by Laura Ingalls Wilder. Her stories of nineteenth-century pioneer life, told from the perspective of the little girl experiencing the Great Plains, have won the hearts of millions. For a time, the Ingalls family lived in Kansas, on a farm near Independence. Bill Kurtis, respected television journalist and host of A&E crime and investigative television shows, owns the property with his sister, Jean Schodorf. Generations of his family lived on those rolling prairies as well, and when it was discovered that this was the site of one of the Ingalls family homes, their cabin was reconstructed. It has become a mecca for fans. The popularity of this site and other Ingalls family homes in the Midwest skyrocketed with the success of the television show, which starred the late Michael Landon and was based on the books.

Michelle Martin is the director of the Kansas Little House site and is a professional historian as well. She has extensively researched the pioneering lifestyle that defined the Great Plains during the nineteenth century, and music played a significant role in those challenging times:

As the wagon train circled and pulled in close for the night the weary pioneers readied for their evening meal. After fires were lit and salt pork fried and biscuits warmed, they reclined to enjoy their evening respite. The crackle of the campfire and its warm glow fortified their spirits along with a good strong cup of coffee. As crickets and coyotes created nature's symphony, the sweet strains of a fiddle filled the night air. Soon the mournful notes

"Pa's fiddle" at the Little House on the Prairie Museum in Independence, Kansas, which interprets the life of the Ingalls family during their time in Kansas. *Little House on the Prairie Museum.*

of a harmonica joined and little by little from all over the camp other instruments joined the impromptu concert. A concertina from one wagon, a guitar from yet another and a twangy banjo blended with nature's night music. Soon once tired men and women sprang to their feet and danced. Singing in different languages, the gleeful pioneers danced their daily cares away despite the barriers of language and culture that otherwise separated them during daylight hours. On the overland trails during the nineteenth century, suffering, struggle, and music were shared in common by all who made the arduous journey west.

In the nineteenth century music was an integral part of life for many Americans, both those born here and those who braved the dangerous ocean crossing looking for a better life. Church hymns, Negro spirituals, sacred harp singing, work songs, and songs of leisure were important forms of communication, expression, and creativity for Americans who did not have our modern forms of entertainment. Young ladies were most assuredly expected to learn and master the playing of at least one instrument to make herself the exemplary Victorian woman. Immigrants arriving on American shores brought with them their unique forms of musical expression and once here made them a part of the American musical experience. In frontier communities one could hear fiddles, banjos, concertinas, guitars, klezimers, dulcimers, pianos, and bagpipes coming from churches, taverns, shops, and homes. Music was the glue that held people together and gave them happiness in good times and comfort when times were bleak.

One of America's most beloved children's authors, Laura Ingalls Wilder, chronicled the importance of music in her pioneer family's life in her classic Little House *series. Written in the 1930s, Wilder's works reflected back upon her family and their rootless pioneer life from the late 1860s to the 1880s when they finally settled in the town of DeSmet in Dakota Territory. For Laura and her sister[s] Mary, Carrie and Grace a cherished memory was when their father Charles took out his fiddle and played for the family's entertainment. In* Little House in the Big Woods, *set near the town of Pepin where the family lived before and after their brief sojourn to Kansas, Laura wrote:*

"When the fiddle had stopped singing Laura called out softly, 'What are days of auld lang syne, Pa?'

"'They are the days of a long time ago, Laura,' Pa said. 'Go to sleep, now.'

"But Laura lay awake a little while, listening to Pa's fiddle softly playing and to the lonely sound of the wind in the Big Woods...

"She was glad that the cozy house, and Pa and Ma and the firelight and the music, were now. They could not be forgotten, she thought, because now is now. It can never be a long time ago."

For Laura some of her fondest memories of childhood centered around [sic] *the stillness of the night broken by the sweet, melancholy strains of Pa's fiddle playing in the darkness as she drifted off to sleep. Millions of readers and later television viewers fell in love with the music of Pa's fiddle and the wisdom that he often times dispensed in front of the family fireplace while playing. Today, those who yearn for the past can visit Laura's home in Mansfield, Missouri, and once a year hear the sounds of Pa's fiddle fill the air when it is gingerly removed from the museum's showcase and played for adoring crowds. No matter how hard we try, we cannot escape our nineteenth century music and cultural past.*

The stories shared by Laura Ingalls Wilder repeated themselves across the plains of Kansas hundreds of times over. Little museums across the state bear witness with the tarnished brass instruments or the fragile fiddles and the yellowed sheet music that bore the popular tunes of the day.

10

NO PLACE LIKE HOME

Kansas has one of the few state songs recognized around the world. With simple, expressive lyrics and a tune that encourages a sing-along, "Home on the Range" is sung by every school kid in the nation and has been recorded by countless artists. It began with a modest cabin in Smith County.

In 1871 or 1872, Dr. Brewster M. Higley wrote a poem about the tiny cabin where he lived in north central Kansas, not far from Nebraska. He called the poem "My Western Home" and tucked it away as nothing special. A neighbor found the poem and convinced Higley to share it with others. It was first published in a December 1873 issue of the *Smith County Pioneer* with the title "Oh, Give Me a Home Where the Buffalo Roam." Fiddler Dan Kelley helped set the poem to music, and the song soon acquired a life of its own.

As Americans fell in love with the simple song, they added verses and the chorus. There was no "home on the range" in Higley's original poem. The song became an icon of the American West, and in 1947, "Home on the Range" was named the official state song of Kansas.

I was leading a tour in the northeastern corner of the state a few years ago, and the overlook in White Cloud was one of our stops. The vista is breathtaking. The bluff over the Missouri River offers a view of Nebraska, Iowa and Missouri. There was a reverent silence, and then the group spontaneously broke into song—"Home on the Range."

The tiny cabin on the bank of West Beaver Creek where Higley penned that poem is still standing today, in the yard of a private home. The property

(Left to right) Chris Frost, Stuart Yoho, Dave Houser, Preston Miller, Kim Houser and Teresa Tucker perform Dave's winning entry in the songwriting contest at the Walnut Valley Festival, Stage 2. *Courtesy Dave Houser.*

has been preserved and can be visited by the public thanks to the Ellen Rust Living Trust. The trust was started by former residents of the adjacent home. The cabin is kept unlocked and has a small exhibit inside, behind chicken wire. There is also a guest register, and they sell a handout with the history of the cabin and the song for a quarter (on the honor system—this is Kansas, after all).

The Higley Cabin was in need of restoration, and in April 2011, a campaign began to raise nearly $100,000 for that work. In the first month, over $25,000 was raised, the bulk of that money coming from a concert by cowboy singer Michael Martin Murphey. The benefit concert was held at the Prairie Rose Chuckwagon Supper Club in Benton.

To reach the Home on the Range Cabin, drive north of U.S. Highway 36 on Kansas eight miles and turn west on the private drive where you see the stone sign.

Home is a recurring theme for Kansas songwriters.

Kim Houser played drums in the band Borderline with Marc in a baby carrier on the floor beside her. His dad, Dave, was just a few feet away on guitar. More than twenty years later, Marc has returned home after a stint in the air force and is the band's leader. He has brought a new dynamic to the band that watched him grow up. Like his dad, he is also a songwriter. Dave won the songwriting competition at Winfield with his song "Driving Spikes," which sounds like a bluegrass classic.

For Marc's inspiration, he turned, not to history, but to the iconic Kansas image in the *Wizard of Oz.* The classic film has been a mixed blessing to Kansans, portraying the landscape in black and white and judging it, therefore, boring. For Kansans brave enough to embrace the film and let their imaginations run, Oz is within reach! My friend Paul Miles Schneider of Lawrence penned the novel *Silver Shoes*, based on the premise that the events had really occurred. For Marc, the guise of Dorothy was the perfect subject of a song that was really about another girl.

"The first girl I was very truly in love with moved from Kansas to Colorado with her dog," he said. "We talked about how he loved it so much and it was amazing and so I paralleled it to the Wizard of Oz to hide up it being directly about her." Marc is in the process of recording this one, and I predict it will be a hit.

"We Miss You in Kansas"

Little girl, where will you go
Walking down an endless road
Don't you know you're far from home
Is that dog gonna keep you from feeling alone
What were you running from
Your stories just begun
We miss you in Kansas
We watched you slip away
How is it girl, in that different world
I hope it's not dull and gray
Your friends are all loving and smart
I see a coward in your heart
Good friends can be hard to find
You seem to lose them all the time
Don't put your love on a shelf
Take a look at yourself
We miss you in Kansas
We watched you slip away
How is it girl, in that different world
I hope it's not dull and gray
You know I hate to see you cry
I'm no wiz, but sure I'll try
To show you a path back home
Where you should never feel alone
And I can tell honestly

That you'll never forget me
They miss you in Kansas
They watched you slip away
It's time girl to give home a whirl
I hope it's not dull and gray
There's no place, there's no place like home
There's no place, there's no place like home
There's no place, there's no place like home
There's no place, there's no place like home

II

THE KANSAS
SONG PROJECT

Cally Krallman and Diane Gillenwater are two of the most unpretentious women in the world, though they have every right to put on airs. Accomplished in so many fields and disciplines, they have contributed mightily to the culture, and pride in the same, in the state of Kansas. The Kansas Song Project is the culmination of their combined talent and energies, and it is an incredibly rich expression of this state's compelling history, but it is also a reflection of their love and passion.

"In the fall of 2002, during a major change in my life, I started writing song lyrics," said Cally. "One of the subjects I was drawn to was Kansas history and particularly from 1850 to the 1890s. The biggest problem with my songwriting endeavor was I did not play an instrument. I had recently seen Pastense, a local bluegrass band, perform at a coffee shop in Topeka. The fiddle player, Diane Gillenwater, was exceptional. I knew her father, a fellow artist. So I called Diane and arranged to have coffee with her, to meet her and share my recent writings. We immediately clicked, and she looked at the 'song' and said that with a few changes, she thought she could set it to music. I started taking fiddle lessons from her. But after a brief time it was apparent that my instrument of choice was the pencil!"

Cally chronicled their partnership on the Song Project's website:

> So I decided to focus on writing. I began to accumulate a lot of lyrics about Kansas and we decided to take it a step further and this was the birth of "Prairie Glimpses—The Kansas Song Project." We felt this could be a

great way to promote Kansas history and inspire others to check out different people and places in our state.

We began to talk to music friends of ours and asked them if they would be interested in either singing or playing on the CD. I had written lyrics for about 22 songs but we eventually narrowed it down.

Several initial tracks were recorded by Mitch Rosenow, Banded Moon Arts & Media, Lee's Summit, MO. As a Kansas native, Mitch was very supportive of the project. His encouragement and involvement early on were instrumental in the project becoming a reality. As time went on, travel became difficult for some of the artists and we eventually moved the recording to the Exceptions Studio in Topeka owned by Randy Wills.

Diane was also in transition when Cally called her, having just been laid off from her job at a local television station.

"I decided to try teaching private music lessons at my house, teaching alternative styles of violin, like bluegrass and Celtic music," recalled Diane. "I knew that if I was ever going to make my living doing what I loved, this was the time. The minute I declared myself a teacher the students started coming. Cally was one of the first ones."

Music was always a part of Diane's life, and she chronicled her musical journey on the Song Project's website:

My first memories of music is my dad playing records of classical music and Broadway shows. My mother, Shirley Meek, had been a music major at Washburn and my father, Fred Meek, had been an art major at Washburn. His father, my grandpa, had been a musician, having his own vaudeville show and traveling the northwest circuit. My uncle George had a great record collection of Sousa Marches [but] my favorite [record] was Alvin and the Chipmunks. Because of my roots it's no surprise that I've been a musician all my life. I learned piano first, because my parents both played. Then when I was in the fourth grade you could pick an instrument to play in the school strings/band. We had a violin that my mom had used in college, so that was how I ended up playing the fiddle. Interestingly enough later on I discovered that my mother's grandfather had also been a fiddler…

I never did get to play the kind of music I wanted on the violin with the exception of playing for musicals. I played in/for many different musicals for various groups around the Topeka area. The good thing about musicals is that I got to play a lot of different musical styles. Finally, after turning twenty-six, I was able to meet up with some people that played Bluegrass

Music. As I mentioned, The Nitty Gritty Dirt Band's music was the style that spoke right to my heart.

It was kind of a soft rock/bluegrass style. That was how my journey into Bluegrass Music began. I had to figure it out for myself because there were no local instructors in roots style music in the area. I played with a couple of different bands before joining up with the bluegrass band, Pastense in the summer of 1995. We have since recorded three CDs. I have become a fairly good bluegrass fiddler and I won the Kansas Fiddling and Picking Championship in 2002.

"All this leads up to the style of music I composed for the Kansas Song Project," said Diane. "I have been influenced by so many great artists over the years. I love the acoustic sound. I have used guitar, fiddle, mandolin, piano, dobro, and banjo in different configurations. I wanted this CD to have a totally acoustic sound. I wanted a common thread running throughout all the songs. A sound like playing in your living room, or being at a family gathering where several people played instruments and sang songs together."

"I composed most of the songs with the help of the performing artists assisting in the arrangements," she continued. "I felt that I did not want to compose all the songs on the CD because I didn't want everything to sound alike. I also wanted to allow the other performing artists to have ownership in the arrangements of the songs. I stayed open to what other people might be hearing in the music and what strengths they brought to the songs. It was important to me from the start that we were all bringing something special to the project and that we would all leave our own mark on the songs. That is what is so special about this first CD."

Diane commented on this collaboration:

We are all Kansas musical artists and we all have grown up here and been influenced by things from here. We have all stayed or returned here and bring all of our experiences to our music. We want to leave a lasting piece of history to those to come after us about how it was for us in our time, especially musically. We have included many songs about Kansas history. We weren't able to live through those experiences so we had to learn about them from the people who did live through them and wrote about them. Now we have taken what we have learned, put it in words and music, that added the emotion that we experience when hearing and reporting these stories.

Cally Krallman (left) and Diane Gillenwater (right) were recognized by Governor Kathleen Sebelius (center) for their Kansas Song Project. *Courtesy Kansas Song Project.*

The songs aren't written to sound like the time period they happened in. They are in real time. Our time. I hope that in a very small way I am creating a future for those who come after me. I hope that we are preserving in this CD a testimony to all those who settled here, who live here now, and those to come in the future. Kansas is a beautiful, unspoiled state rich in history and rich in opportunity. I hope this CD makes you proud to be a Kansan. I also hope that you will listen to it more than once and let the music and the words soak into your soul. To some extent it is honoring those who experienced the unimaginable to us these days. They came through the experience and are still teaching us today. Better yet, put the CD on in your car or truck and take a ride through the Kansas countryside as you listen to the songs. Enjoy.

The four-year project was released in the spring of 2007, and the CD is still available at outlets across the state and online.

Among the performances of the project was the very special evening with the Topeka symphony.

"I will never be able to truly convey my feelings of hearing our music, first written in my living room, then performed by the Topeka Symphony and a bluegrass band on the same stage together," said Diane. "It was truly one of the greatest moments of my life."

Each of the songs represents such a unique moment in Kansas history and a cross-section of the Kansas landscape. Each is a story unto itself, and the musicians who made the recording interpreted these pieces with such commitment to the overall project that it is reflected in their performances. The songs and the personnel who worked on each of them follow.

"Prairie Glimpses"

"Since I am a landscape painter," said Cally, "primarily in Kansas, I was inspired to write this song to 'paint' an image of what I see in the wonderful prairie. I use a lot of imagery in this song…colors, textures, sounds, etc."

This song was composed by Diane and recorded by Pastense.

"What Jacob Reilly Saw"

This is a true story Cally ran across in a man's diary documenting the raid of Quantrill on Lawrence. The story told of a boy who lived on Camp Creek who was kidnapped and forced to lead the ruffians into town for the vicious slaughter of Lawrence residents. The only modification Cally made was to give the boy a name (in the story he was unnamed). Jacob Reilly is a fictional name she gave to the frightened boy.

This song was composed by Diane (also on fiddle and mandolin) and arranged/performed by Michael Paull and Terri Laddusaw of Lawrence and Randy Wills on piano/bass. Judy Coder also recorded this song.

"Farmer's Bride"

"This fun little song is inspired by my days on a farm in western Kansas," said Cally. "As a farm girl, I wondered whether it was my destiny to be a farm wife. My parents had other ideas for me! In reminiscing what those days of what a farmer's wife would have been like, this song was born. Unlike traditional jobs, the farmer is often up before sunrise and then out doing chores until well after dark. It can be a lonely life, and the song is about a farmer who is questioning whether his 'girl' can tolerate this kind of life."

Diane composed the music.

"MILL CREEK ROAD"

This beautiful 'coming home' song was inspired by a road I travel on frequently to find material for painting. It is west of Topeka, in Wabaunsee County. I pretended to be a songwriter living in Austin, Texas. I imagined the twelve-hour drive coming home to Kansas and all the emotions one would feel when returning to one's childhood home. I often feel these emotions when I travel back to western Kansas to see my mother on the family farm. The yard light would often be on, the folks knowing I would be arriving late. The family dog would come barking out to the road to greet me.

This was composed and performed by Terri Laddusaw. The cool part is Diane and I had already played with a very similar composition, and it was as if Terri could read our minds! It felt like a cosmic synchronicity was taking place. Playing piano on this piece is Michael Paull, guitar and dobro was played by Rick Farris and fiddle [was played] *by Diane Gillenwater.*

"ROCK OF EARTH"

This song is about the stone fences all over eastern Kansas. There is a historical marker and a great example of these fences south of Alma on the Rock Hill Ranch owned by Cally's friends Paul and Nancy Miller. She frequently paints out on their ranch. The marker describes how the walls were built out of stones from the fields that farmers needed cleared. The money amount paid for this labor-intensive task in the song is not correct, but she needed a particular word with two syllables. "A writer's creative license," she said.

This song was composed by Diane and performed/arranged by Bob Bowden of Wakarusa.

Oh, Give Me a Home!

"Santa Fe Trail"

The hardships the pioneers faced traveling along the Santa Fe Trail were the inspiration for this song. Cally wanted to describe the "painterly" vistas at sunrise on the Kansas prairie and allow the listener to experience images of pioneer times along the prairie. This song was composed by Diane and arranged/performed by Judy Coder and Pride of the Prairie with Alan Lawton, Stan Tichenor and Phil Thompson.

"Cotton Shirt of White"

This is a story of Lyman Stockwell Kidder, a young soldier sent to meet George Armstrong Custer who, along the trail, was massacred by Indians on the banks of Beaver Creek in northwest Kansas. "I wanted to enhance the story in a way that would symbolize the pain and grief all mothers feel when they lose a son in battle," said Cally. "I embellished the story by having the mother prick her finger as she was sewing on the button before he left for battle, and it left a bloodstain." It was true that the slain soldier was identified by that very shirt. This song was composed by Diane with instrumentals by Ed Farris and performed by Anthony DeLallo of St. Mary's.

"Sunflower Song"

This upbeat little riff was inspired by Cally's nephew:

> During a bout of depression, I was writing a lot of sad songs. He gave me a song challenge. "Aunt Cally, can't you write a happy song?" he asked. Well, I saw this as an admirable challenge, so thus began the song that personifies the blooming sunflowers out in a Kansas field. We grow confectionery sunflowers out in western Kansas on our farm, and I have walked the fields many times looking for photo opportunities. The song came from the golden beauty I would see in the rows of blooming sunflowers and how the flowers might think if they were real people. I composed (in as much as a nonmusician can!) the song and Bob Bowden

arranged and did guitar work on it as well as sang lead vocals. My cousin Ronette Rosenow and I sang backup vocals. This is my happy song dedicated to my nephew Shawn Kirby.

"DAMSEL IN DISTRESS"

A pioneer woman, Julia Stinson, inspired the song. A would-be lynching of territorial governor Andrew Reeder was averted by her dressing the governor up in women's clothing and sneaking him out in the middle of the night. A relative of Julia's, Gary Gilbert, shared the story with Cally and loaned her the book describing Julia's exploits. It is a fun true story that makes a rabble-rousing song. It was composed by Diane and performed and arranged by the Alferd Packer Memorial String Band out of Lawrence (Lauralyn Bodle, lead vocals and fiddle; Steve Mason, banjo, bass and vocals; Matt Kirby, hammer dulcimer; Mike Yoder, guitar; and Jim Brothers, washboard). In addition to being fabulous musicians, Matt Kirby and the late Jim Brothers are great artists/sculptors.

"BLESSED BE"

This song came about as another song challenge. Cally's friend, C.J. Hiestand, challenged her to write a song about a Catholic church. Having driven by the Cathedral of the Plains in Victoria at least a thousand times over the past thirty years, she thought the challenge was easy enough. "I wanted to tell a heartfelt story of a young couple that became pregnant out of wedlock and decided to marry. They did not want the parish to know, of course. But the beauty of the song is they formed a loving bond, had children and lived and loved a good and happy life in the Smoky Hill Valley. The church served as a source of peace and unity during their marriage and after death, the prairie and church, which they were buried near, became the symbols of the unity. The two spires represented the two souls that united in marriage that day." The song was composed by Diane (also on mandolin and viola) and performed by folk singer Lee Wright from Topeka. Randy Wills is on bass.

"Arikaree Breaks"

"I was raised in Northwest Kansas and had never visited this unique land formation until I started gathering song inspirations," Cally admitted. She is not alone. This unique and remote landscape has been ignored by many fellow Kansans. The land near St. Francis is relatively flat and then, from out of nowhere, appear the deep valleys and gorges near the edges of the Kansas/Colorado/Nebraska borders known as the Arikaree Breaks. "Legend has it they don't graze cattle much in this area, because the cows just sort of disappear and are difficult to keep track of," said Cally. "So I imagined this fictional little girl named Katie (after my Aunt Kate) who is quite a little cowgirl. A storm rages in from the west and the cattle get out and she and her horse go chasing after them. Like all mysterious legends, she disappears into oblivion, never to return. I think this was representational of a time in my life when I felt a little lost." The song was composed by Diane (also on fiddle and mandolin) and performed by Terri Laddusaw and Michael Paull. Randy Wills is on bass. (Note: Don't go looking for her tombstone—it's not there!)

"Walk, My Brother"

This is a factual song about the unique town of Nicodemus, Kansas, the first all-black town in Kansas founded during the "Exoduster" era. The once thriving town struggles to survive, like so many western towns, having lost population to the cities. This song was composed by Lemuel Sheppard from Pittsburg and is performed a cappella along with backup vocals from Ed Brunt from Lawrence. "We hope this song will bring awareness to the community and the wonderful people who still live there," said Cally. Nicodemus has been named a National Historic Landmark.

"Prairie Straight-Line Wind"

"Kansas wind, what Kansan is not familiar with this?" asked Cally. "I always said they invented the 'bad hair day' in western Kansas where the straight-line winds have been known to move one county's topsoil to the next county over!" she joked. "But it is this same wind that blows the blades of the windmills on farms and ranches throughout the state to pump essential water to livestock. The storyline for the song, 'Some days I get to thinkin', I may just take up drinkin',' was a common [phrase] I heard many times from my rural neighbors when the wind would blow for days on end."

And of course, no Kansas song would be complete without mentioning the ever elusive "jackalopes." This song was composed/performed by Michael Paull (guitar) with backup vocals by Terri Laddusaw. Diane is on fiddle and mandolin. Randy Wills is on bass.

"FLY AWAY-AMELIA'S SONG"

Perhaps the most famous daughter of Kansas, aviator Amelia Earhart, inspired this song. This poignant song is a synopsis of Amelia as a young girl in Atchison, where she was raised primarily by her grandparents. "She is gazing into the big blue skies over the Missouri River, telling her grandma she would love to be up there flying," said Cally. "Then she fast-forwards to when she is flying around the world with her co-pilot, Noonan, and her plane goes down. This song is a tribute to Amelia, who has been a role model for young women in Kansas and all over the country." This song was co-composed by Cally and Bob Bowden and performed by his daughter Teresa Bowden. Back-up vocals are by Terri Laddusaw. Diane is on fiddle, and Randy Wills is on bass.

"WOMAN OF THE SOJOURN"

"[In this song] Cally describes the pioneer women giving up everything they had or wanted to follow their husbands' dreams of going west," said Diane. "As I took her lyrics and put them to music, I tried to capture how it would feel to do this. It must have been very hard to leave everything you had owned, known and loved behind to do this. It would take nerves of steel and endurance beyond what I would risk to knowing what I know she would have had to endure. I had originally composed it for guitar, mandolin, bass and fiddle, but then Randy worked in some piano to help the Faris brothers with the feel of the song. It sounded so right for this song that we left the piano track. The piano seems to add a lot the emotion. Terri Laddusaw adds to the vocals in this song and you can hear in her voice, one woman, alone but strong. Those women were so brave, so devoted, so strong and because of them I had a future.

"I hope when people listen to this song, they remember those women who sacrificed in order to settle the West," added Cally. Jolleen Thorpe also performs in this one.

"Ghost of Susan Fox"

Cally says: "As Diane suggested, this is the perfect music for a ride through the diverse Kansas landscape, and it always reminds me of those who came before. As a historian, all the songs appeal to my sensibilities, but the 'Ghost of Susan Fox' just touches me on so many levels. Kansas has been home to many soldiers over the years, and this story is such a poignant testament to the experience of love and loss in a soldier's family."

It was inspired by an article Cally found in *Kansas* magazine. Susan Fox was one of the supernatural stories shared around Halloween during the seasonal ghost tours. She was reported to haunt Fort Riley "She was engaged to be married, but her fiancé was called to help care for those with cholera. She contracted it while he was away and died there alone," Cally said. "They buried her in her wedding gown. I wanted to describe what she would have been wearing and the surrounding area. Cottonwood trees in a rural setting seemed to fit." This song was composed by Diane and performed by Terri Laddusaw and Michael Paull. Diane is on fiddle and Randy Wills is on bass and piano on the recording.

"Ghost of Susan Fox"

The daughter of an officer—Susan Fox had raven hair
Her skin was like a cultured pearl—her presence filled the air
The young Fort Riley soldier—Back in eighteen fifty-five
He'd asked Susan for her hand—She was to be his bride
The cholera was plaguing—Many towns across the plain
Her fiancé was called to help—Ease suffering and pain
While out on ordered duty—Young Susan fell ill at home
He didn't make it back in time—and She died there all alone

93

Chorus:
Now the leaves of the cottonwood—Fall gently to the ground
The ghost of Susan Fox—Forever wanders all around
Searching for her true love—She had to leave behind
Her journey to another world—For which she was denied
Her dress was sewn in crinoline—in which she was to be wed
He took out the lacy veil—And he placed it on her head
They buried her across the draw—From the home of her birthplace
He bid her his sweet goodbyes—As he kissed her on the face
She couldn't travel on—to the darkened other side
The fort became the special place—Susan Fox would now reside
They tried to send her on to—Heavens pearly gates
They tore down the old homestead—but of course it was too late
REPEAT Chorus 2X

12

SIX-STRING JUSTICE

Just as the Kansas Song Project provided the perfect Kansas touring music, so did the *Six-String Justice* CD of Dave Zerfas. His lyrics tell the story of the Wild West and the Kansas that was at the heart of the cowboys and Indians, cavalry, railroads, shootouts and shenanigans. The songs recount the violence of frontier Kansas, with the story of the Bloody Benders, the notorious family who lived near Cherryvale and operated a way station of sorts. Zerf's "Beautiful Katie" is a haunting account of the Benders' beautiful, bewitching daughter who lured travelers to their deaths. When suspicions were aroused, the Benders vanished into history. "Roman Nose" is a tribute to the Cheyenne warrior who became a legend. "Sheridan" recounts the wild and wicked town that sprang up in western Kansas and now is found only in bottles under the drifting sand. "California Joe" is the happy-go-lucky tune honoring the larger-than-life character who scouted for the cavalry, including George Custer. Each of the songs is written and performed by a man who knows, and loves, the history and landscape of Kansas.

Jim Gray, publisher of the *Kansas Cowboy*, a quarterly publication of Kansas history and western heritage events, has shared many of the adventures that inspired Zerf's songs.

"Zerf and I have been traveling the prairie for quite a spell now," said Jim. "When we go on 'Zerfari,' we search out the secret places that are not well [known] but have their own historical significance. Along the way we've picked up a few companions to join in the exploration, like California Joe, Young Buff, Prairie Dave and Kansas Jack."

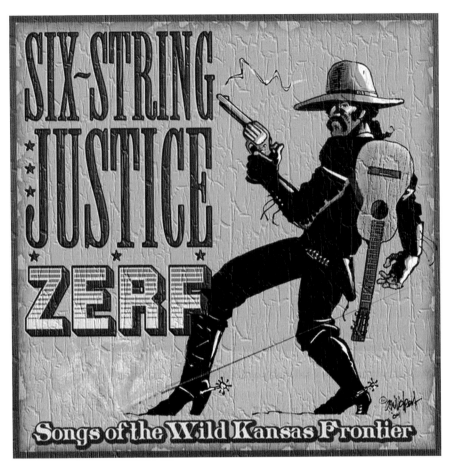

The songs Dave Zerfas has written and performed on this CD are based on the history of the Wild West in Kansas. *Courtesy Dave Zerfas.*

"Zerf brings his guitar, which adds to the magic," said Jim. "I call him the 'Troubadour of the Plains.' Zerf is a tuneful storyteller. Many of the places we have visited turn up in his music and his connection to those places is evident in the haunting lyrics that always get to the heart of the subject at hand. There's nothing more natural than a cool Kansas breeze and the fusion of Zerf's guitar and voice with the wonderfully historic past."

13

MISTER ROGERS

He is probably the most popular substitute teacher in the school district. When he strolls into the jam at Speck's Bar and Grill on Sunday afternoon, the kids yell, "Mister Rogers!"

That's Dennis, not Fred.

The kids recognize him from school, from the library, from Railroad Days, from powwows and from Apple Festival. There is hardly a busier performer on the Great Plains. When his schedule allows, he tours with the multi–platinum selling country band Blackhawk. On numerous occasions, his dance has accompanied the song "Seminole Wind" performed by John Anderson in concert. He has appeared with Willie Nelson and Neil Young in the Farm Aid concerts.

When he was a student at Haskell Indian Nations University in Lawrence, Dennis was a member of the Haskell Singers and Dancers, students representing tribes from one end of the country to the other. They toured across the country as well, taking the culture of their tribes to other areas. After Haskell, Dennis transferred to Washburn University, where he studied education. He has made a career of both educating and performing.

Dennis headed to Phoenix for a couple years, landing a job entertaining tourists at Rawhide, a popular destination. It was there that he learned to "hoop dance," using hoops to create the illusion of animals and dancing through them, around them and with them.

As Dennis performs, dancing or playing flute, he shares stories from his Navajo culture. These are hardly lectures. The traditions and

Navajo Dennis Rogers interprets American Indian traditions in dance and art throughout the Midwest and tours with the band Blackhawk. *Deb Bisel.*

values of his tribe and those of other American Indians is almost a subliminal message as he interprets old ways into new songs and dances. The children are mesmerized, but the parents are not far behind them.

The first time I met Dennis he was sand painting.

"You always draw the eyes first," he said as he swirled the sand. "That's how the spirit enters the painting."

The art is temporary, like the dance—there for only a moment before it is shifted to be shaped again. Like the dance, no two are ever the same.

14

THE PRAIRIE ROSE
CHUCKWAGON

Nestled among ranches, cattlemen and horsemen in Butler County is the Prairie Rose Chuckwagon. The complex has several buildings—theaters, museum, performance hall, barn—situated on the prairie near Benton. As the customers find their seats, they shake hands heartily and say, "Hello, you ole sidewinder!" and, "Why, you ole rascal!" Many wear cowboy boots and hats, not as a fashion statement, but because it is part and parcel of their lives.

"Beef! It's what's for dinner," quips Orin Friesen, leader of the house band, the Prairie Rose Rangers and manager of the establishment. He adds that a lady called to inquire about vegetarian dinners. He replied, "All the cows we serve are vegetarians!" Owners Greg and JW Johnson welcome everyone with a big sign that says, "Howdy!" When the serving begins, all three help the staff carry the hearty meal of brisket, sausage, potatoes, beans, biscuits and apple crisp with ice cream to the three hundred guests assembled for a night of good food, entertainment and fellowship. Yes, fellowship is the right word.

This is a venue where the flag is honored and grace is said.

On this particular night, the entertainment is provided by Roy "Dusty" Rogers Jr., and the crowd is excited. The spittin' image of his dad (except for being a few inches taller), Dusty takes the legacy of Roy Rogers and Dale Evans very seriously. He sings the cowboy songs they made famous, and he sings a tribute to his dad. The crowd loves him, and they love this venue.

Many folks are regulars and come to celebrate birthdays and anniversaries. One couple this night has been together for fifty-nine years.

The Prairie Rose Wranglers obtained permit Number One to perform at the Great Wall of China. The legendary Johnny Western was the lead singer. *Courtesy Orin Friesen.*

There are also tourists from Illinois, California, Ohio, Colorado, New Jersey, Iowa—someone shouts he hails from the "state of confusion." The crowd roars. There are international visitors as well; tonight, a family from China. It is a happy group sharing a communal meal, welcomed warmly and made to feel like family.

JW said their mission is "to provide wholesome environment and entertainment by promoting the good, old-time values of the American cowboy: belief in God, Country and family."

Greg and JW, along with their son, Colton, have a deep love of the old West and a genuine desire to keep the spirit of the American Cowboy alive—today and for many years to come.

As owners of the Bar J Ranch, they not only raise and sell horses but also produce rodeos. They were the first to bring the Ladies' Professional Rodeo to Kansas and co-sponsored the U.S. Army "Support Our Troops" Championships in 2006. This successful business provides them with the means to support and assist worthwhile charitable organizations like St. Jude Children's Research Hospital, the Titanium Rib Foundation, the Muscular Dystrophy Association, the Institute of Logopedics and the Emmaus Mennonite Church Rebuilding Fund.

The entire evening is one of celebration, as intended. One price gets wagon rides, popcorn and a western movie, the cowboy museum, dinner and entertainment. People amble about, comfortable. There is a feeling of wholesomeness and wholeness.

"Those who visit the Prairie Rose become a part of the family throughout their stay," said JW, "and we are forever beholden to each and every guest who comes through our gates."

A lot of people say that. The Johnsons really mean it. They encourage guests not to get a babysitter.

"Bring your whole family—the kids, grandma and grandpa, brothers, sisters. They'll all enjoy the great entertainment here at the Prairie Rose," JW said.

15

THE CELTIC FOX
AND EMMA CHASE CAFÉ

Janet Sage and I went to the Celtic Fox to meet some of her other friends. So many adventures begin at the Celtic Fox.

There was a gorgeous gal singing lead in the band, lots of talent and lots of energy. But it was the guitar player, Glenn Leonardi, who caught my attention. The next morning, I posted on Facebook, "That's the best picking I've heard since I came to Kansas!"

My friend Sue Ann Seel saw that post and sent me a message: "You must be a bluegrass fan." And thus, our relationship was cemented.

Glenn is not a bluegrass player, though he can play anything he wants, I'm sure. It was my reference to him as a "picker" that tipped off Sue Ann. She came over to my house, and we listened to music, tapped our toes and sipped tea, all the while reveling in finding a kindred spirit. She invited me to Cottonwood Falls, to the jam at the Emma Chase Café.

The Chase County courthouse, situated on a hilltop at the end of Main Street, dominates the landscape. It is an ornate structure, in the fashion of late nineteenth-century buildings. It might remind you of a wedding cake.

This particular Friday night jam was devoted to gospel music. I felt a twinge of disappointment. I had hoped for something upbeat, though I enjoy gospel. I needn't have worried. Just to get the crowd in the mood the first song was "I Want to Be a Cowboy." Then there were rousing renditions of Hank Williams's "I Saw the Light," then "I'll Fly Away," then "Do Lord" and "When the Saints Come Marching In." There were softer tunes, too, like the one that Clarence, the newcomer from Wichita, performed—"Let the Harvest Go to Seed."

Nothing goes with traditional music like traditional food. The menu boasted fried catfish, chicken-fried steak, cherry pie, peach pie and rhubarb pie. As the customers came and went, there was barely an empty seat to be had the entire night.

Seated next to me was a young couple with a darling little girl. He was a native of Hamburg, Germany, and was teaching anthropology at Wichita State University. His wife was Turkish. This was their first trip to Cottonwood Falls, and Emma presented them with a jar of apple butter since they had come, the farthest. (Technically, they had driven only from Wichita.)

Driving home that night, Sue Ann and I tried to carry on a conversation, but I had brought along some of my favorite bluegrass CDs, and we kept interrupting ourselves with, "Oooh, listen to this!"

The Friday night jam at the Emma Chase Café was voted as one of the Eight Wonders of Kansas Customs by the Kansas Sampler Foundation.

16

THE LITTLE GRILL
AT THE LITTLE APPLE

On another night, Sue Ann invited me to the Little Grill, located below the dam at the Tuttle Creek Reservoir near Manhattan. Her music teacher Chris Biggs had a semiregular Wednesday night gig with his friend Steve Hinrichs.

I had met Chris. Everybody in Kansas has met Chris, some under more pleasant circumstances than others. A lawyer and politician, Chris was the district attorney in Geary County for several years and then served as securities commissioner before becoming secretary of state. He is now in the Shawnee County District Attorney's Office. More importantly, he has consistently placed near the top at the Flat-pick National Guitar Championships in Winfield. Unlike Chris, Steve, his partner, chose an honorable profession, nursing. I was eager for the jaunt to the "Little Apple."

The Little Grill is owned by folks from Jamaica, and jerk chicken is a favorite on the menu. The décor is beach themed. The ocean may be a bit far, but the Tuttle Creek Reservoir has nearly thirteen thousand acres of water when Kansas is not suffering a drought. Kansans make the most of the state park surrounding it.

Chris and Steve played rock 'n' roll classics by Bob Dylan, the Stones, the Allman Brothers and, here and there, a bluegrass classic like "Sitting on Top of the World" or "Rocky Top." They performed some originals, such as "Send Me to Glory in a Gladbag," written by Chris's big brother, John. Some of Chris's originals were included, such as "Courthouse Blues," based on his experiences as the Geary County district attorney. Its catch

Dixie Lee Jackson and Dave Houser get ready for a performance at Welcome Home Leavenworth. Steve Tennant is a key organizer of the annual event to welcome the new crop of officers to the Fort. *Karen Knox.*

line is "Do I look like Monty Hall to you?" Another crowd favorite is "Devil Woman." No need to explain the inspiration for that one. I was inspired. I began making notes, and when they lit into, "Take Me in Your Lifeboat," I felt the sudden urge to fry tenderloin and make red-eye gravy. It was that moment that Dixie Lee Jackson's *Guide to Cookin' and Kissin'* was born.

My alter ego had been born a year before. Libraries throughout the nation were revisiting *To Kill a Mockingbird* as their "Big Read." My neighbor, library bigwig Susie Marchant, called and asked if I would present a program on southern food. I said, "Sure!"

As the time drew near, I had second thoughts. How boring would it be to listen to me talk about food? I called Susie back and asked, "Is it OK if I do a character?"

The Little Grill at the Little Apple: A Love Story

Kenrick and Cathy met when Cathy was on a vacation in Cancun, Mexico. Kenrick, originally from Montego Bay in Jamaica, was singing at the Beach Palace resort when he met Cathy. A spark was lit instantly. The next night, they walked and talked for hours along the beach. After months of courtship and trips by both to spend time together and meet each other's families, Kenrick romantically proposed.

Kenrick arrived in the States in December 1998, and the two were married on February 2, 1999. The marriage took place in a quaint little restaurant/bar near the local state lake. Among the many family and friends who were in attendance was the building's owner Tootie McCoy. While congratulating the new couple, McCoy disclosed her plans to rent the building in the near future. Kenrick and Cathy had discussed opening a restaurant together and decided to go for it. They opened their doors in February 2002 with ten tables and several chairs they purchased doing side jobs. They had also collected many "island inspired" décor items to give the place the feel and atmosphere they had dreamed of. Kenrick entertained and sang at a tiny stage in a corner, quickly creating a fan base that became part of their regular customer base. All the food was prepared on a "little grill," thus inspiring the name for their restaurant now known throughout the area as the Little Grill. Full ownership of the land and building was obtained in 2009. By word of mouth, business flourished and required expansion and growth of the facility, which now comfortably seats over ninety guests.

The current newly expanded kitchen, dining room and covered patio has provided different sections for Kenrick to entertain his guests. Many fellow musicians are now booked weekly to provide guests with a variety of live entertainment.

—courtesy of the Little Grill

I chose the most feminine southern name possible and visited the Topeka Civic Theatre's wardrobe department for a BIG red wig. There it was, almost hidden behind the other hairpieces. The staff grabbed a ladder and retrieved it for me, and it has been Dixie Lee's trademark ever since. That library program was a huge success with more than two hundred people showing up to watch Dixie Lee make sweet potato sonker and dish out love advice. She has been busy ever since, mostly emceeing music events.

It has been Dixie Lee's pleasure, on many occasions, to introduce Chris Biggs and Steve Hinrichs to appreciative audiences. So well received are their performances that it has been suggested that Kansas revamp its voting laws so that the best banjo player should be declared governor.

It could work.

17

ANDY McKEE

In late 2006, acoustic guitarist Andy McKee burst onto the global guitar scene with a solo acoustic video of "Drifting." The video went viral on YouTube, achieving millions of views by early 2007. Andy, who dropped out of high school to devote time to the guitar, earned his living teaching the instrument. (He later earned his GED.)

According to a 2010 interview in *Premier Guitar*, McKee is one of the most important guitarists to come along in a very long time:

> *As an artist, he represents change and innovation. We used to gauge an artist's popularity by album sales—which, of course, were often dependent on big-label backing for proper production and promotion in order to stand a chance. McKee made his mark with a video camera and an internet connection. The modern metric for gauging what the public is connecting with—YouTube views—is hard to comprehend when you consider McKee's numbers: the total YouTube views for his videos are approaching 100 million.*
>
> *But then again, when you consider his artistry and sheer originality, those numbers start to make sense. Who among us hasn't seen a bearded and dome-shorn McKee slap-hammering that rhythmic tapestry of tones in his "Drifting" video?* [More than 55 million views] *And who can't remember their own reaction to first seeing McKee's wonderfully arranged and skillfully played version of Toto's "Africa"? In a world where awestruck music fans quickly copy and paste URLs to share music videos that impress them, McKee is a reallife* [sic] *digital sensation.*

Andy McKee has become one of the most accomplished guitarists in the world. *Jason Dailey*.

His videos were the top three rated YouTube clips of all time at one point. Though tremendously talented, McKee's time spent woodshedding is just as prodigious. A dedicated student of the instrument who is largely self-taught, McKee learned a lot by teaching, too, and continues to do so when he can. He has won and placed high in numerous fingerstyle competitions around the world. He now plays alongside the world-class players he used to look up to as mentors. His name carries plenty of weight on its own, though, as I can attest after seeing him wow an appreciative crowd with a solo show at the Montreal Jazz Festival earlier this year. Today, with his "day job" behind him, and several more releases under his belt (solo records, as well as discs with Josh Groban, Lee Ritenour and Don Ross), he's a literal "road warrior," playing hundreds of concerts per year—including opening several shows for Eric Johnson and Dream Theater.

Andy's genius is undeniable.

PART II

The Kansas Music
Hall of Fame

Sisyphus believed he could tackle that rock one more time…and that's the kind of faith you have to have in yourself and your work.
—Dawayne Bailey, composer, Chicago **XXXII**: Stone of Sisyphus

18

THE KANSAS MUSIC HALL OF FAME

The Kansas Music Hall of Fame was founded in 2004 to pay "overdue recognition to the many talented and deserving artists produced by the state of Kansas," said board president Allen Blasco. Induction ceremonies and performances are held each year at the former Red Dog Inn, now Liberty Hall. Members of the hall of fame and inductees vote on nominees.

The organization's president-emeritus and founder, longtime radio personality Bill Lee, commented that he is always blown away by the incredible talent represented by the honorees. It was primarily through Bill's efforts that the organization was born, and he hopes that a museum will eventually be established honoring its members. An avid collector, Bill was well on his way to assembling the collection of artifacts that would be the foundation for other contributions when a fire destroyed the apartment building in which he lived. His collection, much of it irreplaceable, was gone. Bill said he lost around two thousand albums from Kansas and Kansas City bands, about four thousand singles and several hundred CDs and tapes. He also had rare live recordings dating to the late 1950s.

It was a setback for Bill personally and for the KMHOF, as well. The annual induction ceremony, however, has not missed a beat—literally. The 2015 ceremony marks the tenth anniversary of the event.

The induction and concert held by the KMHOF has the feel of a family reunion as musicians gather from the corners of Kansas and from the places music may have taken them—Nashville, Los Angeles, Las Vegas, Austin, Chicago, New York. Middle-aged guys run to embrace their old band mates

as if they were schoolgirls. They reminisce, swap stories of the road and recall friends who have passed away. They delight in the opportunity to make music with one another once more.

Since its inception, the KMHOF induction and concert has been held at Liberty Hall on Massachusetts Street in Lawrence. Back in the day, it was known as the Red Dog Inn, and it was one of the most popular venues in the Midwest. It was also home base for many of the bands being booked by John Brown's Mid Continent Entertainment. There is also an open jam with the inductees at the Holidome in Lawrence on the Friday night prior to the KMHOF ceremony. Often, musicians return to the hotel after the ceremony and play into the wee hours.

Evan Johnson, who performed with the Red Dogs, Central Standard Time and the Group, chose a career in business but welcomes the opportunity to see old friends and band mates and to have the opportunity to just be a fan.

"It's a great opportunity to see groups perform that we never saw back in the day since we were all playing different venues at the same time," he explained. "It's also a chance to meet those players and get to know them."

"In addition, it's a reunion of many great friends and former band mates—a way to reconnect after so many years apart—to share memories from some of the most amazing times in our lives," Evan said. "KMHOF also gave several groups (including mine) the chance to re-form and perform again. What a thrill for us lucky old guys! The credit goes to Bill Lee and the

Opposite: Mike Kelley was brought to the microphone by KMHOF founder and president emeritus, Bill Lee. *Beth Meyers*.

Above: Johnny Neal was a multiple inductee into the KMHOF. *Beth Meyers*.

KMHOF Board for making all of this possible. Will never be able to thank them enough."

The late Johnny Neal felt the same way when he returned to Liberty Hall for a reunion of Jerms in 2006. The band that Bill Lee called "Topeka's answer to the Beatles" were Highland Park High School buds, and they had not played together in thirty-five years. Johnny said they picked up where they left off.

"It was magic," Johnny was quoted in the *Topeka Capital Journal*.

Inducted the same year was Spider and the Crabs from Manhattan, and Don Wierman agreed that even after a hiatus of thirty-seven years, the band went right back into the Chicago and Blood, Sweat and Tears covers that had made it so popular.

When Burlington Express was inducted, Blair Honeyman echoed those sentiments. "The opportunity to see people I haven't seen for thirty-five or forty years, the opportunity to reconnect," Blair said, "brings back great times. The 1960s and 1970s were a great time to live."

He also talked about their history as a band.

"We were never a garage band," he remarked. "We were working musicians every weekend for five years. Our first gig (as the Mods), was the grand opening of the Hampton Car Wash on South Topeka Boulevard, in 1965."

Honeyman was also a member of Morning Dew, another hall-of-fame band, but left a music career and has worked for Sherwin Williams in Kansas City for more than thirty years. Performing onstage with his friends once more brought back "a flood of emotion."

Bruce Lyn echoed the sentiment that the band reunion was the best part of the induction. "It was an amazing night," said Bruce Lyn. "We had not played together for forty-two years. To be able to play with those guys I had grown up with—I had not seen Mike West since 1970."

Bruce added that drummer Eric Larson was ill and unable to perform for the induction and Phil Ehart of Kansas filled in. Larsen died a few months later. He was grateful that Eric had lived long enough to see the band inducted.

"It was a great honor," he said.

Lyn's band mate in Burlington Express Greg Hartline was also a member of White Clover. He has been a professional musician in Las Vegas for seventeen years and came back to Kansas for the chance to join old friends on stage.

The KMHOF gives musicians the opportunity not only to reminisce but also to reflect. Johnny Isom became emotional during his acceptance

Donny Weirman thanks the fans at KMHOF induction ceremony. *Beth Meyers.*

speech, which visibly affected the crowd. The accomplished guitarist recounted the time spent hospitalized as a child with spina bifida. Playing guitar gave him a way to excel and to fit in.

"I believe my life has a purpose," Johnny told the audience, "and that purpose is to play music."

In 2004, the late Greg Thompson began writing his memories of his band days, a time in his life that meant so much to him, though his career would be made elsewhere. His dad had an old Stella six-string guitar and played in bands around Wichita. Greg recalled, "He taught me to play the chords to 'You Get a Line, I'll Get a Pole, and We'll Go Fishin' in a Crawdad Hole.'"

Greg's first band was the Dantes, and his recollections are not only his personal story but also the evolution of some of the most popular bands in Kansas during that era. His story is their story and describes how so many of them wound up working as musicians.

"A friend of mine from school, Lonnie Johnson, had an electric six-string and knew a few chords. I was playin' dad's old Stella. Lonnie and I started learning a few songs. We wanted to copy a group called the Fleetwoods; a good vocal group in the late '50s and early '60s. Unfortunately, neither of us sang very well."

Greg turned his attention to learning the bass, a rig he purchased from Sears. He and his friends played their first gig at the Crestview Rec Center in Topeka.

"We played the same four or five songs over and over. Man, we thought we were hot stuff. We needed a drummer and found another guy at school.

Johnny Isom performs at his induction into the KMHOF. *Deb Bisel.*

His name was Dave Newman. He was our age (twelve or thirteen years old) and had a full set of Ludwigs. Dave was from California and had been playing drums since he was old enough to sit on a drum stool.

"We got pretty tight for three punk kids," Greg continued, "but we needed a singer bad. We went through lots of guys. Seems like we had a new singer every few months. We tried whoever could sing whatever was hot on the radio. Finally, we picked up John Neal. John was a few years older than Lonnie, Dave and myself and had played with several local bands."

"John was a lead vocalist and played the keys," Greg wrote. "Not long after John joined us, Ron Mikkelson (who had been with the top Topeka band, the Argons) also joined us as a lead vocalist and playing the saxophone. Things were looking up. We played as a 5-piece group, The Dantes, for another year or so."

As transitions go, Lonnie left the band and a new player joined the group, Bob Brennan. The group dynamic was trending more to R&B, and it was becoming more solid. So the band members auditioned for John Brown and Mike Murfin at the Red Dog Inn. They were offered a job as one of the Mid Continent bands, along with the Flippers, the Red Dogs, Spider and the Crabs and the Blue Things.

"John Brown gave us the name The Rising Suns (we later became the Young Raiders)," Greg wrote. "The Rising Suns were actually pretty much the Dantes. The original Rising Suns consisted of John Neal (vocals and keys), Ron Mikkelsen (vocals and sax), Bob Brennan (guitar), Dave Newman (drums), and me—Greg Thompson (bass)."

The band toured the Midwest playing towns like Central City, Nebraska; Yankton, South Dakota; and Plano, Texas. It performed in National Guard armories and at universities. Greg recalled that the Righteous Brothers were a big influence and that Ron Johnson and John Neal had the ability to harmonize like Bill Medley and Bobbie Hatfield.

"By this time," Greg wrote, "we had the B3 organ, the brass section, the vocals, and the experience to create a sound that we had been looking for."

The Young Raiders were inducted into the KMHOF in 2009.

Two brothers who have been inducted into the KMHOF, not as band mates, but with separate groups, are Daniel Edward and Phillip Lincoln Smith.

"Three of the five surviving Smith kids chose to be musicians," said Dan, who was inducted with the band Riverrock. "I was fortunate to meet the right people and start Riverrock, which has dominated my involvement in music for forty years. My youngest brother, Phil, who can play circles around me on a drum kit, sing better and make me laugh, besides being a talented visual artist, left Glow [inducted in 2014] and Kansas City behind to become a much-in-demand drummer in L.A."

"In between us is our brother, Steve, who knows more about music than Phil and I combined," continued Dan. "Steve has a master's degree

The current incarnation of Riverrock is pictured at Kaw Point in Kansas City. *From left to right*: Allen Blasco, Paul Mumma, Dan Smith and John Mumma. *Courtesy Dan Smith.*

in orchestral music from Northwestern University, and he has been the conductor for the Olathe Community Orchestra since 1985, received a 'Founders Award' as a conductor for Theatre in the Park in Shawnee Mission, has taught high school orchestra for almost thirty years and plays sax and violin in several KC bands, including AnnaLee and the Lucky So & Sos. Riverrock and Glow are in the Kansas Music Hall of fame, but brother Steve belongs there, just on his own merits."

The band Sanctuary was inducted in 2014 with Eric Bikales returning from Nashville to join his former band onstage and visit family and friends. He spent many years in Los Angeles, where he worked with the likes of Mike Post. He continues to perform with Neil Sedaka. No matter who he performs with, however, he reserves the highest praise for those early band mates.

"These guys are more than the best musicians; they're the best people around. [I] can't believe I got to play in a band with all of them," he said. "Getting inducted not only validated Sanctuary for all time but [also] allowed us to relive the experience one more time."

Kansas has one of the few halls of fame for which the members vote on the inductees, an opportunity truly reflecting the organization's commitment to honoring the fans' choices. Membership information is online at ksmusichalloffame.org, and KMHOF maintains an active Facebook page.

THE KANSAS MUSIC
HALL OF FAME INDUCTEES

The decision over whether or not to include the list of inductees from nine years was difficult. First, it will change; each year, there will be new names added to the list. Second, the list is not balanced. Some inductees have far more detailed bios than others. This does not reflect on the bands or individuals in any way; rather, it reflects the limitations of the board and organizers who just cannot possibly know everyone. Much of this information sprang straight from the memory banks of Bill Lee, and bless him for writing it down. It speaks to the strength of the organization that there is such variety of genres represented. It also speaks to the challenges of a volunteer organization in dotting all the i's and crossing all the t's. It is so important to remember the accomplishments of Kansas musicians that I decided it was better to use incomplete information than to leave any of the inductees out, and to use this opportunity to extend the request for memberships, information and photographs. If you see oversights or omissions, or you just have more information to share, please contact the KMHOF board. This organization is in its infancy. If this volume has demonstrated anything, it is the absolute fact that the state of Kansas has, is and will produce incredible musical talent.

Something that will become obvious as you peruse this list is that there is much crossover between the bands. The evolution of band personnel is just the nature of the beast. Many times, though, you might be shocked to note the longevity of some of these groups or the number of years many of them have devoted to a single band while maintaining an active music life in other pursuits. Each of these artists has an incredible story. Folks like David "Bubba" McKown, who grew up in Great Bend but now makes his home in Hawaii, are so full of information on the music and bands in the western part of the state that it begs for another book. So many stories, so little time!

2014

Ed Down, Lawrence, Directors Award

Ed Down started the Audio House Recording Studio in 1951. The company was originally located in his house, hence the name Audio House. His specialty was on-location recording. He recorded concerts for colleges, public schools and music camps, selling records of the concerts as souvenirs for the students. Ed invented a way to imprint album covers so he could do small batches of records at a reasonable price. In 1962, Audio House recorded the soundtrack for the movie *Carnival of Souls*, produced by Herk Harvey, which has since become a cult classic. (The movie was filmed at Lawrence locations, the Lecompton Bridge and in Salt Lake City, Utah.) Ed was an accomplished disk-mastering engineer, adding stereo mastering capability by 1969. He made a point of hiring women who were trying to get back into the work force after raising a family and, by 1977, had ten full- or part-time employees. In January 1978, Ed had a heart attack, dying peacefully in his sleep.

Clif "Rockin' Daddy" Major, Wichita

Clif Major began a lifetime of soulful and stylistic guitar mastery as a child in the 1950s. Among Clif's bands, discography and achievements are the Outcasts (band), "South Wind" (1983 winner of the Telluride Bluegrass Competition), the Del Reys (band was given a five-star endorsement in *Guitar Player* magazine) and the Jukes (band). He owned C Major Guitars & Banjo's and opened C Major's Rockin' Daddy's, a cabaret, in 2004 with Kathy Roush Major. In 2013, a Wichita State University special collection was established as the "Clif Major and Kathy Roush Music Collection," consisting of their collective music history and memorabilia, intended for regional music history research. Clif passed away in June 2014.

Glow, Kansas City

Formed in 1977 by John Kessler (keys and vocals) and Philip Lincoln Smith (drums and vocals), Glow (originally named Checkmate) created a powerful blend of original progressive rock, jazz fusion and pop music. Guitarist Brian Milam joined in 1978 and propelled the band into the public consciousness with his incendiary chops. Bassist Paul Davis joined in 1981. All the members contributed to the band's compositions, but it was the song craft and compositional daring of Kessler and Milam that proved most successful. Various other great musicians were part of Glow, but the four-piece group of Kessler, Milam, Smith and Davis is remembered as a "musician's band": uncompromising, fearless and unique. Glow took first place in the KY102 Best of Home Tape competition in 1983, was a finalist in the Miller High Life Rock-to-Riches contest and was also on KKCI's *Moonshine II* LP. The band's original music attracted the organizers of the 1984 Montreux Jazz Festival in Switzerland, and that summer, Glow performed in front of enthusiastic audiences on two of the festival's stages.

Beast, Hays

The Hays version of the Dinks was looking for a new direction and a chance to get into the recording studio. Dick Dole (promoter/agent) contacted Michael Kerns (flute/sax) from Colorado to move to Hays and join the Dinks. Michael's band from Colorado, Beast, had dissolved, so the Dinks decided to pick the name up and became Beast of Hays in 1970. The band consisted of Michael Kerns, Dean Dietz (lead vocals), Bruce Brown (bass/vocals), Donnie Wierman (guitar/vocals), Mike Schmidt (drums) and Dana Messing (keyboards/vocals). They played over a twelve-state area in the Midwest for a period of four years. Beast had three recording sessions: two in Clovis, New Mexico, under Norman Petty (in the same studio used by Buddy Holly), plus a later recording session in Boulder, Colorado.

Sanctuary, Lawrence

Sanctuary was formed in 1971 in Lawrence by Dennis Loewen, lead singer and mastermind of the Fabulous Flippers. In association with Mike Murfin, Dennis, along with Minneapolis singer-songwriter phenomenon

Roger Bruner, teamed up largely to do original material. Both Dennis and Roger were already accomplished performers. At this point, Norman Weinberg (drums) and Eric Bikales (flute and keyboards) joined the team, and Sanctuary was born.

"One of the most compelling things about Sanctuary was the message in its music. Both lyrics and music were always heartfelt and honest," recalled Bill Lee. "This was a time and a generation that stood for ideals and making a better world, which is in part why Sanctuary had such a large and devoted following. With incredibly captivating performances—charismatic, powerful and distinctive—Sanctuary was one of a kind."

The Wichita Linemen

The Wichita Linemen formed in October 1969 and played their first dance in November 1969 at the NCO Club on McConnell Air Force Base in Wichita. During their thirty-year career of playing dances and shows (mostly in Kansas), they averaged over two hundred performances per year, playing from Wichita, north to Nebraska, south through Oklahoma, east to Kentucky and Tennessee and as far west as Los Angeles. In the beginning, there were two disc jockeys in the band from KFDI radio station in Wichita: Don Powell (steel guitar) and Don Walton (vocals). Greg Stevens (bass guitar, banjo, saxophone, keyboards, harmonica and fiddle), Carl Hendricks (lead guitar) and Robin Harris (drums) rounded out the band. All members were vocalists. This was the original group that played "in the rowdy milieu of The Western Swinger," a Wichita nightclub. In the ensuing years, keyboards and fiddles would be added, and various other great musicians would pass through the ranks. The Wichita Linemen's last dance and show was New Year's Eve 2000 in Ruidoso, New Mexico, with the Charley Daniels Band.

In his book *Goat Glands and Ranch Hands: The KFDI Story*, Orin Friesen addressed the issue of the band's name. "[Greg] Stevens claimed the name was chosen several months before the release of Glen Campbell's smash hit 'Wichita Lineman' in one of the most fortuitous coincidences in country music history." Orin cited another band member, Robin Harris, who said the band chose the name right after the song came out, and commented, "You can't copyright a song title—we could have called ourselves White Christmas."

Jimmy Dee & the Fabulous Destinations, Victoria

When filmmaker George Lucas directed the movie *American Graffiti* during the 1970s, he could not have predicted the wave of nostalgia that swept the United States as a result of the smash hit. It was during this time, in 1975, that a group of musicians from Victoria formed the group Jimmy Dee & the Fabulous Destinations. Little did those musicians know that their high-energy show, featuring major hits from the early 1960s, would propel the band into one of the most popular groups to ever perform in western Kansas. Forty years later, the band is still going strong, playing selected dates throughout the year with tremendous fan support.

Donnie and Diane, Arkansas City, Bob Hapgood Award

This brother-and-sister act from southern Kansas sang together at their mother's insistence and encouragement. They honestly couldn't understand why people responded to them, but respond they did. When songwriter Bill Post returned from California, he took an interest in the two youngsters, producing a record entitled *Hotrod Weekend*, which climbed into the regional top ten and received national airplay. A few years later, Donnie and Diane Harper won Wichita radio station KFDI's talent contest. First place was a recording session, and they recorded "Little Bitty Mini Skirt," which reached number eleven on KFDI'S music charts. Donnie and Diane set attendance records at local fairs and shows and were very well known in the southern Kansas–northern Oklahoma regions. An album was released in 1972 and was rereleased on CD in 2013. Bonus tracks include all their singles, plus many unreleased gems by the duo, including six songs with Conway Twitty and the Blue Boys.

The Bon Ton Soul Accordion Band, Kansas City

Inspired by zydeco accordion legends Clifton Chenier and Rockin' Dopsie, Richard Lucente rediscovered his long-abandoned childhood instrument on extensive travels in Creole Louisiana. Soon after, he was afforded the opportunity, at age forty, to start his first band. Lucente's prolific songwriting skills enabled the ever-evolving band to present an adults-only, dance-friendly original blend of zydeco, blues and R&B to its considerable and rabid fan base. It also supported the release of five successful albums composed totally of original songs. The band's annual Crawfish Fiestas routinely drew ten thousand fans. The band's induction into the 2014 Kansas Music Hall of Fame is dedicated to the late, great Ed Toler, bassist for seventeen years of the band's existence.

Junior Brown, Lawrence

"With his unique voice, more unique songwriting craft and even more unique invention (the double-necked 'Guit-Steel'), there has absolutely never been anyone like Junior Brown," said Bill Lee. He's had a major label signing (Curb), a Country Music Association (CMA) Award, three Grammy nods, a Bluegrass Music Association Award (with legend, Ralph Stanley), duets on record and video appearances with everyone from Hank Thompson and George Jones to the Beach Boys and Stone Temple Pilots. Movies, TV shows, commercials and multiple appearances on late-night TV have punctuated his career. There was even a cameo appearance on *SpongeBob Squarepants*. Born in Cottonwood, Arizona, his first major musical employment was with fellow KMHOF inductee Billy Spears in Lawrence.

2013

Devastating Dinks, Salina

This successor to the original Dinks was based out of the Lamplighter in Salina and initially included a member of the first Dinks, but the new band was soon very much its own band and took the name to new heights, playing all over the western half of the state and surrounding states between 1968 and 1970.

Exceptions, Topeka

The Exceptions are one of the longest-standing, most successful, pop-variety bands in the Midwest performing all styles of music. Randy Wills, Craig Senne and Tom Ingles founded the band in 1966, but Tom was soon replaced by Steve

Steve Greene was not a founding member of the Exceptions but joined soon after the group was formed. *Deb Bisel*.

Greene. Marta Barron recalled that she was the first female vocalist for the group. She and her husband, Ric, were part of the Exceptions for two decades. Other personnel included Kim Murphree, Forrest Bethel, Lynn Blackwell Nehf, Lisa Thomas, Corey Wilson, Thom Thomas, Pete Larson, Jake Jacoby, Martin Hale, Lisa Sato, Tim O'Reagan, Tom "Chip" Cipolli and Mark Wangerin.

Ray Hildebrand, Prairie Village

Ray Hildebrand smashed onto the music scene in '63 with the number-one hit "Hey Paula." Ray wrote the song that he and Jill Crawford, dubbed Paul & Paula, recorded while in college in Fort Worth. Paul & Paula followed up with "Young Lovers" and five other songs in the Hot 100. Ray became one of the founders of contemporary Christian music. He traveled for the Fellowship of Christian Athletes as a speaker and performer and later became a youth director for a church in Prairie Village. Ray was a frequent guest as a singer for the Billy

Ray Hildebrand reprised his 1964 hit "Hey Paula" with his daughter at his induction into the KMHOF. *Deb Bisel.*

Graham Crusades. In '83, he hooked up with CCM artist Paul Land. Land and Hildebrand have played together all over the United States and have recorded sixteen albums. Ray still does about twenty-five dates a year.

Kerry Livgren, Topeka

Kerry Livgren was a founding member of the rock group Kansas, whose big hits were "Dust in the Wind" and "Carry On Wayward Son," both of which Kerry wrote. In 1980, Kerry became a born-again Christian and left Kansas to form the contemporary Christian music band AD. He later became a solo artist. Kerry lives on a farm near Berryton and records in his home studio.

Chuck Mead, Lawrence

After leading the Blinkies and Homestead Grays in his hometown of Lawrence back in the early '80s, Chuck Mead landed in Nashville, where he co-founded the country band BR549. The band's name was derived from

Lawrence native Chuck Mead prepares for his performance during sound checks for KMHOF inductions. He now makes his home in Nashville. *Deb Bisel.*

Hee Haw, country's answer to Rowan and Martin's Laugh-In. Each week, the bumbling Junior Samples advertised his used cars for sale and held a cardboard sign with the phone number, BR549. The band's seven albums, three Grammy nominations and the CMA award for Best Overseas Touring Act built a strong reputation. In 2009, Chuck released an acclaimed solo album and continues to tour with his band the Grassy Knoll Boys. He's also the music director of the Broadway smash show *Million Dollar Quartet.*

Mystic Number National Bank, Kansas City

The Bank played so many free concerts and antiwar demonstrations back in the late '60s that it was thrown out of the Musician's Union. Lead singer and drummer Glenn Walters later sang and played with California's Hoodoo Rhythm Devils. He's still playing for crowds in San Francisco in addition to a career singing on TV commercials and film soundtracks.

Playmate Blues Band, Hays

This group was made up of some of the area's best musicians. The band's lineup originally was Mike Kelley (guitar), Gary Cooley (bass), Richard Bisterfeldt (drums) and Bill Seibel (horns). Two of the band members, Mike and Rich, went on to join the last lineup of the original Blue Things. These hard rockers toured extensively on the Midwest ballroom circuit of the 1960s.

Tempests, Hays

This nine-member R&B show band played the Midwest from 1965 to 1968. When the band was playing in the 1960s, the age of the members ranged from twelve to fifteen. They were so young they had to hire college students to haul their trailer and equipment to gigs. After a more than forty-year hiatus, the band decided to reunite to play some shows during Hays High's homecoming weekend. The Tempests practiced for a week and played shows at the VFW for family and friends Friday and for the class of 1971 reunion.

Steve Werner, Kansas City

A uniquely talented, and revered singer, songwriter, guitarist and bandleader, Steve Werner was unforgettable to all who knew him and experienced his music. During the '60s and early '70s, his seminal country rock groups Next of Kin and Bartok's Mountain introduced and defined the genre for many in the greater Kansas City area and beyond. Well into the '70s, he continued to show his versatility in the soul, funk and rock idioms with the formation of the Rhythm Kings, Hotfoot and the self-named Steve Werner Band. Moving to Los Angeles in 1979, he formed the pop-rock band Snapshots, which has been called "the greatest unsigned LA band ever." By the late 1980s and into the '90s, his group Mighty Rusty and the Stumblers allowed him to express his talents in all the aforementioned styles, plus jazz. Leaving music, he became the stage manager for the Hollywood Bowl for a time and then went to work for Disney, where he had an entire wing of the animation department named in his honor. He died at age fifty-one from a cerebral hemorrhage. His sudden and premature death is sad but does not deter from his memorable and lasting musical legacy.

Wizards from Kansas, Lawrence

Originally called Pig Newton & the Wizards, the band changed the its name at the insistence of Mercury Records. Its sound was so similar to that of some of the bands coming out of San Francisco that many collectors and fans still think the band was from California. Its one Mercury album regularly sells on eBay for more than $200 a copy. A reunion a few years ago resulted in a second album.

Junkyard Jazz, Lawrence

Junkyard Jazz has been playing traditional jazz of the 1930s and '40s since 1981. The group plays every Thursday evening at the Lawrence American Legion, attracting musicians from northeast Kansas to join onstage. The dance floor is always full. The band has lost a few longtime members, but the tradition of Junkyard Jazz will never die.

Junkyard Jazz has logged thousands of hours over the decades entertaining their fans. *Beth Meyers.*

Sherman Halsey, Independence

Sherman Halsey is an American music video and television director, producer and artist manager. Sherman has produced and directed hundreds of television shows and music videos for artists such as Tim McGraw, Brooks and Dunn, Alan Jackson, BB King, Michael Bolton, Dwight Yoakam and many more. Halsey began his career in the country music business at the age of thirteen, putting up posters and show bills for his father's (Jim Halsey) management and concert promotion company in the family's hometown of Independence. This would be the start of a father-and-son collaboration that continues in business today as an important part of the country music industry. While studying film at the University of Kansas, Halsey promoted concerts with artists from the Jim Halsey Company's roster, such as the Oak Ridge Boys, Freddy Fender, Hank Thompson, Don Williams and many others. During his time at the university, Halsey worked for Dick Clark Productions in Beverly Hills one summer on the NBC Special "The Wild, Sensational, and Shocking '70s." As a result of this experience with Dick Clark, he built relationships with several veterans, network directors who taught him the art of directing and producing.

Larry Emmett & the Sliders, DeSoto

The Kansas City area's first homegrown rock band of note was Larry Emmett & the Sliders. Larry was a Native American, born on the Prairie Band Pottawatomie Reservation near Mayetta. His parents moved to DeSoto, where Larry attended high school and began playing the guitar. In the late '50s and early '60s, the band played gigs from Kansas City to Omaha and many points in between.

2012

Bloodstone, Kansas City

The sweet soul sounds of this R&B group took us on a "Natural High" to *Billboard*'s Top 10 in 1973. The group was influential in the "black rock" and funk movements of the 1970s with its many hits, charting thirteen songs between 1973 and 1984. Since leaving the charts, the band's members have returned to make their base in Kansas City, where they started out in 1962 as the Sinceres.

Burlington Express, Topeka

The Burlington Express was one of Topeka's top bands in the mid- to late '60s. Members of the band were Greg Guecker, Blair Honeyman, Eric Larson, and Mike West. They left behind some excellent recordings, but they sounded even better live. Lead guitarist Greg Guecker, now known as Greg Hartline, wrote most of their material, but they also covered other songs of the day.

Max Carl, Lawrence

Max Carl Gronenthal is an American rock singer, keyboardist, guitarist and songwriter. He is the current lead singer of the classic rock band Grand Funk Railroad. In addition, he spent several years as the keyboardist and lead singer with 38 Special, for whom he co-wrote and sang the hit song "Second Chance." Among his earlier bands was Lawrence's Fabulous Flippers.

Clocks, Wichita

The Wichita-based Clocks arrived on the pop rock scene in 1982, and they almost immediately made an impact on the local music scene. They left us one of the most identifiable songs from that era. The band flourished a bit with the launch of MTV, as their video for "She Looks a Lot Like You" received some decent airplay. It showcased the band's signature keyboards with a hint of new wave vibe. Their CBS/Boulevard single and self-titled album both charted nationally.

Cole Tuckey, Lawrence

This band was put together to open Lawrence's Off the Wall Hall in the fall of 1975. Led by guitarist Allen Weiss and featuring singer/violinist

Dynamic fiddler Janet Jameson is captured on stage at Liberty Hall. *Deb Bisel.*

Janet Jameson, the band was soon known for its original songs and exciting live performances. There were a few personnel changes over the years, but whatever the lineup, Cole Tuckey never disappointed the crowds that came to its shows. Eventually the band broke up with Weiss relocating to California. Jameson, already a 2009 KMHOF inductee with Shooting Star, continues to play with that band, Rock Paper Scissors and Nation in Kansas City.

Finnigan & Wood, Wichita

Keyboardist Mike Finnigan and guitarist Jerry Wood teamed up in this band back in the '70s. Their 1972 album, *Crazed Hipsters*, is considered a Midwest R&B/rock cult classic. In 1973–74, another album was recorded but was ultimately shelved when Blue Thumb Records was sold to Paramount. Wood has passed away, and Finnigan was touring during the induction ceremony; instead, Ray Bagby, the group's drummer, gathered musicians for a tribute. Among them was Dennis LaPlant, who played with a Finnigan Wood reunion in Wichita and was part of the Jerry Wood Group. He played with them until 1973, and that next year, he moved to Los Angeles and joined the Mark-Almond Band. The core of the band was from London, England, and played soft rock and jazz. After a while Dennis decided to form another group called the Sass Band, an eleven-piece band that played big-band blues music. With this band, he played with music greats like Big Joe Turner and Big Mama Thornton. Then, in 1977, Dennis went on tour and became the musical director, bandleader and lead guitarist for the legendary Martha Reeves and the Vandellas, who made such hit songs as "Dancing in the Street," "Heatwave" and "Jimmy Mack." Martha Reeves herself introduced Dennis to her good friend Mary Wells who was popular from her hit "My Guy." From there, Dennis played numerous local Los Angeles gigs with the likes of the Coasters, the Drifters and Mickey Gilley. With many accomplishments under his belt, he decided to tour and landed a job with the world-famous Bob Hope's USO shows. The group played the music for the legendary comic with the funnyman himself, Bob Hope, up front and Dennis, the little boy from Sedalia, on guitar. Together they played for our troops at many air force bases throughout the country and from the Philippines to Guam. Once the tour ended, Dennis went to work on the Jerry Lewis telethons and provided the background music for the various acts. In 1981, Dennis thought he would move back home to Missouri and settled down in Branson. He quickly became busy playing with a band called the Sliders, who played '80s rock 'n' roll covers, and the Ozark Country Jubilee and Truman Lake Opry, where he played country music hits. Gigging six days and six nights a week, he felt he was pushing himself to the limit, so he came to Kansas City. In 1990, he performed with Hank Williams Jr. Kansas City Chiefs football great Derrick Thomas (Ole No.58) had a limousine contract with the PGA tour and wanted Hank to provide the musical entertainment. Derrick knew of Dennis's agent and hooked him up with Hank. Dennis put together a band, and they all played at Bartle Hall. After the gig, Hank asked Dennis to stay on board and play with him for the next six months. Back in

Dennis LaPlant (at podium) was on hand to induct Finnigan and Wood into the KMHOF: Ray Bagby, Johnny Neal, Michael Dee and Bill Lee. *Beth Meyers*.

2010, while in Little Rock, Arkansas, Dennis was at a local venue listening to Bob Marley's band the Wailers and was asked to come up and play with them on their encore song. Dennis admitted he can't remember the song as he was in awe of playing with such a fantastic group. These days Dennis owns a recording studio, Sky High Sound Lab, in Sedalia and still frequents Kansas City. He has signed with Sony to produce film soundtracks.

Johnny Isom, Kansas City

Johnny Isom—or Johnny I, as he has been known since the mid-'80s—is a true representation of the midwestern music scene. Johnny did a couple years in the Kansas City Chiefs band. In the '60s, Johnny put together the Stoned Circus. His current band, the Receders, is a regional favorite.

Krazy Kats, Kansas City and Moberly, Missouri

The legendary Krazy Kats were formed on Valentine's Day 1957, when guitarist Lee Dresser, piano man Willie Craig and drummer Freddy Fletcher, three Moberly, Missouri high-schoolers, decided they wanted to rock and roll like Elvis, Jerry Lee Lewis and the rest of their favorites. Now based in Kansas City, the trio has logged over four thousand gigs together. The group was voted the Best Band in Kansas City in 1991 and was inducted into the Rockabilly Hall of Fame in 1999, and its original songs are included on many U.S. and European compilation albums marking more than fifty years of rock 'n' roll.

Morningstar, Kansas City

Morningstar first formed in 1969. The lineup went through many changes over the years. Its recording contract with Columbia/CBS in 1978 produced two albums. The band seemed willing to play for anyone, anywhere. It opened for other bands and headlined other venues. In the late '70s, disco was going strong, and punk rock had just started to change the musical landscape. Record companies were dropping acts, so after two albums, Morningstar and Columbia/CBS parted ways. Then Morningstar disbanded.

Stanley Sheldon, Ottawa

Stan is a bass guitar player best known for his work with Peter Frampton. He played on *Frampton Comes Alive*, the biggest selling live album of all time. His most recent collaboration was contributing as co-writer and bass player on Frampton's 2007 Grammy winning album *Fingerprints*. He has also played with Tommy Bolin, Ronin, Warren Zevon and Delbert McClinton. Stan was a part of the 2011 Peter Frampton tour.

Tommy Stephenson, Ottawa

Tommy Stephenson, a veteran of versions of inducted bands the Blue Things and the Young Raiders, is a keyboardist with fifteen gold and multi-platinum CDs to his credit. A part of Tommy Bolin's Energy and Joe Walsh's

Barnstorm, he has also recorded or toured with such artists as the Eagles, Eric Clapton, Albert King, the Band, Albert Collins, John Lee Hooker, Paul Butterfield, Gary Wright, Poco, Chuck Berry and many more!

Craig "Twister" Steward, Wichita

Harmonica player Steward played on a couple of Frank Zappa albums and performed live with Zappa's band, as well. Now living back in Wichita, he plays at local clubs and works as the arborist for the city. Hohner Harmonica Company says, "Twister is the Hendrix of the Harp!"

White Clover, Topeka

When Phil Ehart's father retired from the air force, the family settled in Topeka, where Phil started playing in bands. In 1969, he moved to New Orleans for three months, and then he spent three months in England. After his visa expired, he returned to Topeka and formed White Clover. Later, Phil added Sarasota's guitarist/songwriter Kerry Livgren to the fold, and White Clover evolved into Kansas.

2011

Count Basie, Kansas City

William "Count" Basie, who died in 1984, was an American jazz pianist, organist, bandleader and composer. Basie led his jazz orchestra almost continuously for nearly fifty years. Many notable musicians came to prominence under his direction, including tenor saxophonists Lester Young and Herschel Evans, trumpeters Buck Clayton and Harry "Sweets" Edison and singers Jimmy Rushing and Joe Williams. Basie's theme songs were "One O'Clock Jump" and "April in Paris."

The following year, Basie became the pianist with the Bennie Moten band based in Kansas City, inspired by Moten's ambition to raise his band to the level of Duke Ellington's or Fletcher Henderson's. Where the Blue Devils were "snappier" and more "bluesy," the Moten band was classier and more respected and played in the "Kansas City stomp" style. In addition to playing piano, Basie was co-arranger with Eddie Durham, who actually did the notating. During a stay in Chicago, Basie recorded with the band. He occasionally played four-hand piano and dual pianos with Moten, who also conducted. The band improved with several personnel changes, including the addition of tenor saxophonist Ben Webster.

Central Standard Time, Coffeyville

Central Standard Time evolved out of the last of the original Red Dogs in January 1970. Kent Leopold, Evan Johnson, Randy Shaw, Bob Meyerhoeffer, Roger Walls and Richard Tade were all members of the last original Roarin' Red Dogs Band when it decided to leave the Midwest on its quest to make it big in the music business. Since not all of the Red Dogs wanted to make this move, Mitch Bible, Mike Redd and Larry Church were added to the band that would soon become Central Standard Time. Kent Leopold and Evan Johnson were the leadership that landed the band its first gig in Boston in February 1970. Before leaving Kansas, the band changed its name to Central Standard Time.

The original members of Central Standard Time, with instruments played and home town, are Kent Leopold, sax and flute (Coffeeville, Kansas); Evan Johnson, drums (Topeka, Kansas); Bob Meyerhoeffer, vocals and guitar (Hastings, Nebraska); Randy Shaw, drums and vocals (Council Grove, Kansas); Mike Redd, bass guitar and vocals (Wichita, Kansas); Richard Tade, Hammond B-3 and piano (Wichita, Kansas); Mitch Bible, lead guitar and vocals (Mulvane, Kansas); Roger Walls, trumpet and vocals (Rose Hill, Kansas); and Larry Church, trumpet (Wichita, Kansas). Later versions of the band featured Greg Ayers (trombone), Doug Owen (vocals), Jim Doherty (drums), Dave Ferguson (lead guitar), Moose (drums) and Robbie Barker (organ).

James Gadson, Kansas City

Drummer, producer, singer and songwriter James Gadson was born in Kansas City, Missouri, in 1939. As a teen, he took naturally to the drums with the influence of his father, Harold, who was a drummer in the legendary Kansas City scene. James eventually found his way to Los Angeles and joined the legendary '60s funky soul group Dyke & the Blazers, where he laid down drums on "Let a Woman Be a Woman," which later would be sampled by the Bomb Squad for Public Enemy's "Welcome to the Terrodome." After Dyke's tragic murder, and while still in L.A., he and other members of the Blazers would end up forming the Watts 103rd Street Band. With the help of Bill Cosby, they hooked a record deal with Warner Bros. He wrote and sang on some songs like the soulful "Dance a Kiss & a Song." He played on the best-known 103rd Street cuts like "Express Yourself," which was sampled by Dre for NWA's "Express Yourself." This was just the beginning for Gadson's prolific career, which next found him in the mix with Bill Withers producing, writing and playing on the "soul"-cessful *Still Bill* LP, which featured "Use Me," "Lean on Me" and the funky "Kissing My Love," which has been sampled to no end. The Jungle Brothers cut up his drums live for "Straight Out the Jungle." From there, he became one the most sought out studio drummers, playing on three hundred gold records at last count, though you would never suspect it from his ever-humble disposition. He played on Marvin Gaye's "Let's Get It On," the *Saturday Night Fever* soundtrack, Herbie Hancock's *Manchild* and, most recently, Beck, Paul McCartney and Ray Charles discs. Currently he is doing more sessions and is a founding drummer of the Keepintime project with photographer B+.

Rudy Love, Wichita

Rudy Love & the Love Family was a sibling group headed by eldest brother, Rudy. Over the years, nonsiblings performed under the name, but Rudy remained the driving force; Love Family blood members are Bob, Gerald, Peggy, Denise and Shirley. Rudy was born on September 15, 1948, in Oklahoma. Later, the family moved to Wichita, Kansas; it was a large brood—Rudy has fourteen brothers and sisters.

He developed a love for singing and performing from his gospel singing/ musician father, Robert, and went from there. A touring singer, Robert crisscrossed the country as a performing musician with gospel and R&B artists. Rudy became the man of the house while his dad was away playing. Through his father, Rudy met many of the top names in music when they passed through Wichita. He formed his first group in grade school and went through many others before settling on Rudy Love & the Love Family in college. The group performed locally but didn't record.

Pat McJimsey, Wichita

Wichita's Pat McJimsey began heading up bands at the age of seventeen with Velvet Honey. Late, he formed the Bear Valley Blues, the Entire British Navy and Four Brothers. Pat toured with John Manning, Finnegan & Wood, Leon Russell and Freddy King. Upon his death, the PAT (Performers Assistance Trust) was established by the Wichita Blues Society to offer financial help to musicians who cannot play due to major illness, accident or medical emergency or to their survivors to help with final expenses.

Shortly before his death and due to many requests from his fans, Pat McJimsey digitally remastered the *I Dig Girls* album originally released in the '80s. He was very excited about this rerelease and had plans to come out with a new "all blues album" later in the year.

Thanks to the magic of the Internet, and the devotion of his family and friends, Pat's extraordinary talent lives on to be experienced here by old and new fans alike.

Charlie Parker, Kansas City

Charlie Parker was born in Kansas City, Kansas, and was raised in Kansas City, Missouri, an only child. His dad was reportedly an alcoholic and often absent from Charlie's life, though he may have influenced him musically. He was a pianist, dancer and singer on the Theater Owners Booking Association, a vaudeville circuit for African American performers.

Parker began playing the saxophone at age eleven and, at age fourteen, joined his school's band using a rented school instrument. One story holds that, without formal training, he was terrible and thrown out of the band. Experiencing periodic setbacks of this sort, at one point, he broke off from his constant practicing.

It has been said that in early 1936, Parker participated in a "cutting contest" that included Jo Jones on drums, who tossed a cymbal at Parker's feet in impatience with his playing. However, in the numerous interviews throughout his life, Jones made no mention of this incident. At this time, Parker began to practice with great diligence and rigor, learning the blues, "Cherokee" and "rhythm changes" in all twelve keys. In this woodshedding period, Parker mastered improvisation and developed some of the ideas of bebop. In an interview with Paul Desmond, he said he spent three to four years practicing up to fifteen hours a day. It has been said that he used to play many other tunes in all twelve keys. The story, though undocumented, would help to explain the fact that he often played in unconventional concert pitch key signatures, like E (which transposes to C# for the alto sax).

Groups led by Count Basie and Bennie Moten were the leading Kansas City ensembles and undoubtedly influenced Parker. He continued to play with local bands in jazz clubs around Kansas City, Missouri, where he perfected his technique with the assistance of Buster Smith, whose dynamic transitions to double and triple time certainly influenced Parker's developing style.

In 1938, Parker joined pianist Jay McShann's territory band. The band toured nightclubs and other venues of the southwest, as well as Chicago and New York City. Parker made his professional recording debut with McShann's band. It was said at one point in McShann's band that he "sounded like a machine," owing to his highly virtuosic yet nonetheless musical playing.

As a teenager, Parker developed a morphine addiction while in the hospital after an automobile accident and subsequently became addicted to heroin. Heroin would haunt him throughout his life and ultimately contribute to his death.

The Rainmakers, Kansas City

Missouri has long boasted of being the home of two of America's greatest artists, Mark Twain and Chuck Berry. However, it wasn't until the Rainmakers thundered into the national music spotlight in 1986 that anyone combined the guitar power of Berry with the social wit of Twain into a unique brand of Missouri rock 'n' roll.

Originally formed in 1983 as a three-piece bar band known as Steve, Bob, & Rich, these Kansas City rockers became an instant favorite throughout the Midwest. Soon, fans were standing in line to see this trio they described as "energetic" and "intense" but, most importantly, "fun." Within months of finishing their first independent release, Steve, Bob, & Rich had signed a multi-album contract with Polygram Records, added a fourth member and changed its name to the Rainmakers.

Heralded as "America's Great Next Band" by *Newsday*, the Rainmakers were soon drenched in critical acclaim. Feature articles in *Newsweek*, *Rolling Stone*, *CMJ*, *USA Today* and others poured in, singing the praises of this hardworking Midwest band that provided new life to a traditional rock format.

Critics particularly enjoyed the unique writing style of Bob Walkenhorst, whose talent for choosing unusual and sometimes controversial subjects provided an eye-opening perspective of life, sprinkled with sarcastic humor. The

Rainmakers received notoriety for their songs' lyrical content, including Music Connection's award for Lyric Line of the Year—"The generation that would change the world is still looking for its car keys"—and in the unlikely source of author Stephen King, who twice quoted lyrics from Rainmakers songs in his bestseller *The Tommyknockers* and again in his 1991 novel, *Gerald's Game*.

But success did not stop at the U.S. borders, as European countries supported the band increasingly with each new release. The song "Let My People Go-Go" gave the Rainmakers their first Top 20 single on the British charts. Critics abroad sang the band's praises, with feature articles in *New Musical Express*, *Kerrang*, *Rock Power* and others. Frequently, the Rainmakers could be spotted on European television with live appearances on *Top of the Pops* and *The Tube*, as well as from video play on MTV Europe.

European concert dates grew in number each year, with the Rainmakers often enjoying headline status on festival bills. Their reputation as an electrifying concert act eventually led to the recording of a live album at a sold-out show in Oslo, Norway, for release solely in Scandinavian markets.

In 1990, after four albums, five videos, more than 500,000 records sold and concert dates too numerous to count, the Rainmakers put band business on hold to allow time for their personal lives and agendas. In 1994, the band returned to the studio to record a new album entitled *Flirting with the Universe*, an album that achieved gold certification in Norway within two months of release.

Overwhelmed by the response to *Flirting with the Universe*, the Rainmakers reemerged from the studio in 1996 with *Skin*. With this effort, Bob Walkenhorst has again proved that no subject matter is too controversial by taking aim at pornography and its societal impact via his unique perspectives—a Rainmakers trademark. The album was a release, which in true Rainmaker form, was designed to provoke.

The Rainmakers are Bob Walkenhorst (vocals, guitar), Steve Phillips (lead guitar, vocals), Michael Bliss (bass, vocals) and Pat Tomek (drums)

Riverrock, Kansas City

Riverrock is "one of the most popular bands in Kansas City History," says the *Kansas City Star/Times*. Since 1974, Riverrock has been a name country music fans could count on for an exciting show of hot pickin', tight harmonies and spontaneous fun. The band has shared the stage with dozens of recording stars, such as Vince Gill, Trisha Yearwood, the Ozark Mountain Daredevils,

Riverrock's early years. *Front row, left to right*: John Mumma (with banjo), Steve Hall (with bass) and Dan Smith (with washboard); *back row, left to right*: Paul Mumma (with guitar) and Jim Blanton (with fiddle). *Courtesy Dan Smith.*

Hank Williams Jr., Alabama, Suzy Bogguss, the Oak Ridge Boys, Minnie Pearl, Charlie Daniels, Wanda Jackson, Jerry Lee Lewis, Tanya Tucker, Tracy Byrd and Emmylou Harris. Many of these performances were at state and county fairs, concert halls, music festivals, rodeos, college campuses and popular nightclubs.

Bobby Watson, Kansas City

Best known for his work in the Jazz Messengers and Horizon, this post-bop alto saxophonist has recorded twenty-six albums as a bandleader and plays on nearly one hundred others. He moved home to Kansas City in 2000 and currently serves as director of jazz studies at UMKC. He still manages to balance live engagements around the world with teaching.

Jimmy Wilson, Eudora

Saxophonist Jimmy Wilson has been part of the northeast Kansas music scene for many years, beginning with Larry Emmett & the Sliders in the late '50s. In the '70s, he was part of Lawrence's Used Parts and other groups. More recently, he has spent several years playing in Johnny I & the Receders.

(Left to right) Jimmy "Sweet Lips" Wilson, Gary Bisel, Ric Barron, Johnny Isom and Dave Spritzer (in the foreground) are at the Kansas Hall of Fame, the Great Overland Station. KMHOF inductees are chosen each year to perform for the KHOF ceremony. *Danl Blackwood.*

Chely Wright, Wellsville

Following her debut album in 1994, the Acadamy of Country Music named Chely the Top New Female Vocalist in 1995. Her first Top 40 country hit came in 1997 with "Shut Up and Drive." Two years later, her fourth album yielded a number-one single, the title track, "Single White Female." Firmly established as a performer with record sales well over one million on various albums, she is also a successful songwriter. Her songs have been recorded by Brad Paisley, Richard Marx, Indigo Girls, Mindy Smith and Clay Walker, among them Walker's top-ten hit "I Can't Sleep," which won her a BMI award. Her memoir, *Like Me*, was released in 2005. She is an outspoken advocate for gay rights.

Garth Fundis, 2011 Directors Award

An independent record producer, Fundis's credits include some of country music's cream of the crop: Trisha Yearwood, Keith Whitley, Don Williams, Sugarland, Terri Clark, Alabama, Waylon Jennings and Emmylou Harris, as well as New Grass Revival, Doc and Merle Watson, Sheryl Crow and Townes Van Zandt. He has served as chairman of the board of trustees for the National Academy of Recording Arts & Sciences (NARAS) (2001–03), past trustee and president of the NARAS Nashville Chapter and serves on the boards of the Grammy Foundation and MusiCares, Alumnus of Leadership Music. Fundis owns the renowned Sound Emporium Recording Studios. His project with Trisha Yearwood *Heaven, Heartache and the Power of Love* was released in 2007 on Big Machine Records.

Jesse Stone, Atchison, 2011 Bob Hapgood Award

Born in Kansas, Jesse Stone began performing in his family's minstrel show at the age of four. By the '20s, he was leading a jazz band that included saxophonist Coleman Hawkins, a future jazz legend. Jesse Stone and His Blue Serenaders became a fixture on the Kansas City jazz scene.

Jesse Stone was one of the greatest songwriters of the rhythm-and-blues and rock 'n' roll era. Much of his best-known work was done at Atlantic Records, where he wrote, arranged and played on some key sessions. His "Money Honey," recorded by the Drifters, topped the R&B and pop charts for eleven weeks in 1953 and was covered by Elvis Presley early in his career. Another of Stone's songs—"Sh-Boom," by the Chords—was a doo-wop classic from 1954. "Shake, Rattle and Roll," recorded by Big Joe Turner, Bill Haley and His Comets and many others, became a turning point in early rock 'n' roll history. The song served as a bridge to R&B for white teenagers.

Another standout from the era, "Your Cash Ain't Nothing But Trash," was a hit for the Clovers. As a musician, Stone led the house band on Chuck Wills's rocking update of blues singer Ma Rainey's "C.C. Rider." On the jazz side, he wrote "Idaho," which became a standard. Benny Goodman's version topped the charts, and Guy Lombardo's version reportedly sold more than three million copies. Stone penned "Smack Dab in the Middle," which became the signature song of Joe Williams, vocalist with Count Basie's band in the mid-'50s, and was later covered by Ray Charles. Charles also recorded Stone's "Losing Hand. Other R&B classics written by Stone include "Flip, Flop and Fly" (Big Joe Turner), "Cole Slaw" (Louis Jordan) and "Don't Let Go" (Roy "Hamilton).

2010

Oleta Adams, Kansas City

This popular singer was a regular performer on the Kansas City club scene before being discovered by the British band Tears for Fears. Her platinum debut album *Circle of One* produced her biggest hit, the Grammy-nominated "Get Here," which was the unofficial anthem of the 1991 Gulf War.

The Commancheros, Lawrence, 2010 Bob Hapgood Award

One of Lawrence's early rockers were the Commancheros. Two members went on to play in the Red Dogs while another was a member of Wellington's Fantabulous Jags.

Conny and the Bellhops, Pittsburg

Beginning in 1958, this group spread its brand of rockabilly over the region in live shows and on record. Many of the band's old recordings continue to find fans on European compilations. Lead guitarist Gene Woods died recently in Arma, leaving only one original member, Russell Pryer.

Gary "Igor" Crawford, Kansas City, 2010 Directors Award

The late Gary "Igor" Crawford was a longtime road manager for Mid-Continent Entertainment and eventually became the owner of that booking agency. He later founded AME Entertainment, an agency in Kansas City.

Green River Ordinance, Emporia

The Green River Ordinance began in Emporia as a four-piece and played mostly British music. The Green River Ordinance was the opening act for the Outsiders when they toured through the area in 1966. When the band grew to six members, the style was focused on West Coast rock 'n' roll, including the San Francisco sound. The band toured extensively throughout the Midwest, playing in eight states over the years while advertising gigs on KOMA out of Oklahoma City, including a series of performances in Grand Teton National Park. They were frequent performers at the Red Dog Inn in Lawrence and Wichita, the Store in Emporia, the Fireside Inn in Hutchinson, the Dark Horse Inn in Hays, the Lampliter in Salina, Me and Ed's in Manhattan, the Hilltop Club in Atchison and many other clubs, VFW Halls and armories throughout the Midwest. The band had a reunion recently and is looking forward to another opportunity to perform live for its many fans.

Bill Lee, Lawrence, Special Directors Award

Kansas Music Hall of Fame founder and president, Bill Lee, was surprised at this year's induction show when his fellow board members joined him onstage and announced that he was being inducted into the Hall of Fame for all of his efforts on behalf of Kansas music over the years.

Lee spent twenty-five years as a radio disc jockey and program director, wrote a book about Kansas music in 1999 called *Kansas Rockers…The First Generation* and moderates a Yahoo group devoted to discussing old Kansas and Kansas City music.

Moanin' Glories, Wichita

The Moanin' Glories played a British-flavored R&B similar to the Stones and Rascals from 1965 to 1971. Too good to be confined to Wichita, they toured as far away as Boston and Tokyo before breaking up. Recent reunions have drawn large, appreciative crowds.

Morning Dew, Topeka

The Dew led the Topeka music scene in the late '60s with cover versions of the latest hits and original songs. Their fuzz and feedback were featured on an album released by Roulette Records, which has been reissued several times over the years. Copies of the original vinyl sell for big bucks on eBay. Cicadelic Records of Tucson has two Morning Dew CDs out currently.

Plain Jane, Manhattan

Beginning in 1971, this party band went through personnel and style changes but was always one of the hottest bands around. Based in Topeka, Manhattan and Kansas City over about a decade, the band was led by Jimmy Bond and appeared on the soundtrack to the movie *Zapped*. Bond was later a part of Kansas City's Liverpool, a Beatles tribute band, until his health forced him to drop out a couple years ago.

Pott County Pork & Bean Band, St. Mary's

Favorites in Manhattan, Topeka and Lawrence back in the mid-'70s, Pott County Pork & Bean Band was a hard-drivin' country/bluegrass/rock band. Even with a mandolin and fiddle in the band, the musicians never forgot to rock with a sound that owed a lot to the Dirt Band and the Grateful Dead.

Vernon Sandusky, Edna

This sensational guitarist began his career with Bobby Poe & the Poe Kats in Coffeyville back in the mid-'50s. A decade later, Vernon was leading the

Chartbusters in Washington, D.C., with whom he had a Top 40 national hit called "She's the One." He later joined Rodney Lay's band the Wild West and spent many years playing behind Roy Clark, both on TV's *Hee Haw* and in Branson, Missouri.

Bobby Poe & the Poe Kats, 2009 Bob Hapgood Award

Bobby Poe & the Poe Kats—Rockabilly Hall of Famers from the 1950s—were a groundbreaking act that featured legendary piano player Big Al Downing and renowned guitarist Vernon Sandusky.

Big Al Downing went on to become a number-one country star, Vernon Sandusky was in Roy Clark's band for more than twenty years and Bobby Poe became a successful producer, manager and "tip sheet" publisher.

The Poe Kats were also rockabilly queen Wanda Jackson's touring and/or backing band and various members can sometimes be found on her early singles, including the rockabilly classic "Let's Have a Party."

Tree Frog, Lawrence

"Resonates in any language!" "Hopping back in time!" If you lived in Lawrence in the '70s and you liked bands like the Byrds, Buffalo Springfield and the Flying Burrito Brothers, Tree Frog was the band to see. Known locally for its epic four-hour performances at places like the Lawrence Opera House (now Liberty Hall) and Off-the-Wall Hall (now the Bottleneck), Tree Frog was actually a nationally touring band that was just one big break away from the big time. The band spent a decade on the road playing every college campus and alley bar from Athens, Georgia, to Missoula, Montana. Though Tree Frog disbanded shortly after the disco craze hit, the members reunite every couple years to play at Liberty Hall (the former Red Dog Inn) in Lawrence.

2009

Danny Cox, Kansas City

Danny Cox was born in Cincinnati, but he moved to Kansas City in 1967 and has spent much of his life there. Early musical influences in his life included the church choir, where he sang with Rudolph Isley of the Isley Brothers. His country/folk career began with performing on a Hootenanany Folk Tour. He became a partner in Good Karma Productions with Stan Plesser, who managed the folk rock duo Brewer & Shipley and southern rock band the Ozark Mountain Daredevils. Cox has recorded albums for ABC Dunhill, Casablanca, MGM and other national labels. Fundraisers by fellow musicians helped the family rebuild their home and business that were destroyed by fire. Danny writes jingles and works with children's theater. One of his recent projects included writing the music and lyrics for and starring in *Fair Ball*, a musical based on the experiences of players in the Negro Baseball Leagues.

The Dinks, Beloit

While their two novelty songs on the Sully label are favorites with record collectors, it's their song "Penny a Tear Drop" that was a hit with Kansas fans. Beginning as the Raging Regattas, they became the Dinks at their first recording session in 1966.

Larry Lingle, McPherson

In a long career that took him from bands in his hometown to singing and playing with two bands already inducted into the Hall of Fame (Topeka's Jerms and Lawrence's Fabulous Flippers), Larry spent time in Los Angeles disco bands before spending 1981 to 1993 as one of Frankie Valli's Four Seasons. Larry lives in the Northwest and continues to perform.

Lee McBee, Lawrence

One of the best harmonica players around, Lee gained national attention in the late 1980s and early 1990s for his work with Mike Morgan and the Crawl, and for his band the Passions. These bands toured the United States, Canada and Europe and recorded on major blues labels. Lee died June 24, 2014.

The Sensational Showmen, Concordia, Chanute/Ft. Scott, Parsons/Pittsburg

A succession of bands using this name played in Kansas from the mid-'60's into the mid-'70s. The three lineups who were together the longest and are best remembered by the music fans of Kansas are the ones chosen for induction.

The final version of the group began as a concept in 1968 among several Parsons High School students. Steve Hartman (drums and vocals), Jeff Crane (lead vocals and trombone), Mike Seeley (keyboards, keyboard bass and bass guitar), Randy Cruse (lead guitar) and Mike Young (trumpet) chose the name the Gallery. A short time later, the name was changed to the Great

The Sensational Showmen was one of the most active bands in the Midwest. *Courtesy Chris Cruz.*

The Sensational Showmen joined old bandmates on stage for the band's induction into the KMHOF. *Courtesy Chris Cruz.*

Awakening. Jerry Cruz soon replaced Young on trumpet, and the group began playing local dance jobs. Chris Cruz joined around 1970, playing trumpet and rhythm guitar. Later, Randy Cruse moved away from Parsons and Mike Fitzmorris became the lead guitarist. At a high school dance in Buffalo, the band was approached about assuming the name the Sensational Showmen. Shortly afterward, Tom Broadhurst on bass guitar joined the band. Joe Horton of Parsons filled in for Mike Seeley at times on the keyboard. Andy Oberg of Chanute joined as the regular keyboard player. As the Showmen, the band was contracted by America's Best Attractions booking agency in Kansas City, Missouri, which landed them gigs in a wider geographic area, including military bases in Illinois, Ohio and Kentucky.

The Serfs, Lawrence and Wichita

Formed in 1965 at his Kansas University fraternity house, this was Mike Finnigan's first band in Kansas, but it wouldn't be his last. Mike was inducted into the Hall of Fame in 2005, but the entire band deserves consideration for its blues-based music, much of it written by Topeka native Lane Tietgen.

While recording the band's album for Capitol in New York City, three of the guys were invited to jam with Jimi Hendrix, and they became a part of history when two tracks from the jam appeared on Jimi's *Electric Ladyland*.

Shooting Star, Kansas City

This Overland Park band was on the verge of superstardom more than once during the '80s. Its fresh, original material got it record deals with Virgin and Geffen. Lead singer (Ronnie Platt) has left to join Kansas, but violinist (Janet Jameson) is a standout during performances.

Billy Spears, Lawrence

Fiddler Billy Spears began playing professionally back in the early '50s and traveled with top country acts, including Ferlin Husky, Jean Shepard and T. Texas Tyler, before settling in Lawrence. His bands have included many of

Billy Spears, renowned fiddler, entertained audiences for decades. *Courtesy Bill Lee and KMHOF Collections.*

the area's top players, and many have gone on to successful careers in county music, including guit-steel player Junior Brown. Billy died July 6, 2013.

The Young Raiders, Lawrence

This band took up where the original Rising Suns left off. After losing their equipment in a wreck and giving up the band name, the guys decided to go back out on the road as the Young Raiders. Eventually about a hundred of the best musicians in Kansas would serve time in the band. Many of them are still playing music for a living.

Jim Halsey, 2009 Directors Award

Jim Halsey's career spans over fifty active years as artist manager, agent and impresario, discovering and/or guiding the careers of such illustrious personalities as Roy Clark, the Oak Ridge Boys, Waylon Jennings, the Judds, Reba McEntire, Minnie Pearl, Clint Black, Tammy Wynette, Mel Tillis, Merle Haggard, Dwight Yoakum, the Judds, Lee Greenwood, Hank Thompson and many others. He has organized and presented country music performances all over the world, in many places for the first time. His efforts have expanded the horizons of country music into Europe and Asia, while maintaining one of the most highly skilled and motivated booking and management companies in the world.

Jim Halsey has received many honors and awards; is prominent in business, arts and entertainment; and lectures and teaches extensively at colleges and universities around the world.

2008

Ann Brewer & the Flames, Baldwin City

One of the first female vocalists and bandleaders to affect the rock 'n' roll music scene in Kansas, Ann Brewer was equally at ease singing rockabilly or covering the latest James Brown hit. She later moved to Las Vegas, where she found success until damage to her vocal cords ended her singing career. She now lives in California.

The Classmen, Kansas City

The harmonies of this group, led by the Dimmel brothers, made it a local favorite in Kansas City and across the Midwest. The Classmen's old records bring big bucks online these days from collectors around the world. Their song "Graduation Goodbye" still gets radio airplay each spring.

Big Al Downing, Coffeyville

In a career that stretched from the late '50s until he died in 2005, Big Al had hits on the pop, soul, disco and country charts. See Bobby Poe and the Poe Kats.

The Fabulous Four, Kansas City

Originally formed in 1959 as the Midknighters, the Fabulous Four has been known by a number of names, including the Fab Four, the Next Exit, Kansas City and the Pretty. The band has also recorded for a number of labels such as Brass, Coral, Cavern, Pearce, Warner Bros. and Trump/Capitol, where it had its only charting hit, "Linda Was a Lady." The original band consisted of drummer Alex Love, bassist Bob Theen, guitarist Jeff Mann and keyboardist Mike Meyers. Drummer Mark Higbee would replace Alex Love in a later incarnation of the group. Known for its tight and precise instrumental arrangements and vocal harmonies, the Fabulous Four had a weekly gig at the Combo Club in the Waldo district of Kansas City for many years. Later, it held court at a club in the Valentine district called the Attic, along with parties, clubs and all kinds of events around the Midwest. The band's last gig was in 2007. Guitarist Jeff Mann passed away in 2012, but their fabulous sound will live on.

Friar Tuck & the Monks, Emporia

Out of the western plains, this band moved to Emporia at one point and found the same success it had enjoyed at home. The band was popular at dances all across Kansas.

Garry Mac & the Mac Truque, Kansas City

Garry Mac and the Mac Truque evolved out of another noteworthy Kansas City soul band, American Sound, Ltd. The Mac Truque were Garry Mac (guitar/vocals), Dani Gregory (lead vocals/percussion), Tim Ballard (vocals/trumpet/tenor sax), Buddy Haney (bass/trumpet) and Ray Bagby (drums/trumpet). Many of the band members would play more than one instrument at once, and their performances were nothing short of astounding. Their album, Truqued Up, was recorded live by Capitol Records at the former Ambassador Hotel in Los Angeles in the Cocoanut Grove Lounge and released on the label in September 1969. The LP was produced by Kelly Gordon, who wrote "That's Life" for Frank Sinatra. Gordon also wrote "Along Came Love" for Mac Truque. This Capitol Records 45, paired with a gritty version of "Mickey's Monkey," was their only single. To this day, both the LP and single are prized by soul music fans the world over. For those fortunate enough to see and hear them way back when, Garry Mac and the Mac Truque were simply the best blue-eyed soul band, ever.

Pat Metheny, Kansas City

Pat Metheny played a Wichita jazz festival as a fourteen-year-old, and by fifteen, he was playing with the best in Kansas City. Winner of twenty Grammys in twelve categories (thirty-five nominations), his versatility is without peer on any instrument. (No one else has won in more than ten different categories.) He has performed with artists as diverse as Steve Reich to Ornette Coleman to Herbie Hancock to Jim Hall to Milton to Nascimento to David Bowie. Pat's body of work includes compositions for solo guitar, small ensembles, electric and acoustic instruments, large orchestras and ballet pieces, with settings ranging from modern jazz to rock to classical. He has sold more than twenty million records worldwide.

Chet Nichols, Kansas City

This singer-songwriter, who eventually went home to Chicago, was a part of the Good Karma stable of acts in Kansas City, touring with Brewer & Shipley, the Ozark Mountain Daredevils and Danny Cox before recording his first album for Kama Sutra Records. He works in numerous creative media and is a hands-on media artist. He is an award-winning songwriter, composer for TV/film/commercials, recording artist, multi-instrumentalist, ASCAP songwriter and publisher, music producer, lyricist, entertainer and engineer. He also designs websites and specializes as an interactive (web), broadcast, music, video, live-action, special effects and 3D animation producer. This Renaissance man is also a published novelist and Route 66 historian.

Beth Scalet, Lawrence

This folk and blues singer moved first to Lawrence and then to Kansas City, building a solid reputation for her songwriting and crystal-clear vocals. She passed away on March 16, 2014, in Kansas City.

The Soul Express, Hays

One of the best of the many horn bands in Kansas back in the 1960s, this band was at the top of the heap in Hays. It toured extensively and always drew large crowds. Several veterans of the band continue to perform across the country.

Lou & Betty Blasco, 2008 Directors Award

This couple was a big part of the Kansas City music scene for many years with a music publishing company and a record label and as songwriters. "My Happiness" was written by Betty Blasco and Borney Bergantine and became one of the most popular songs in the country in 1948. At least six different acts hit the charts with it that year, and Connie Francis took it to number two on the *Billboard* chart in 1959. The song has been recorded by hundreds of different artists, and it's also recognized as the very first song ever recorded by Elvis Presley in 1953.

Bill Post, 2008 Bob Hapgood Award

Songwriter Bill Post was the first winner of this award, which was named for the 2006 Hall of Fame inductee and founding member of the Hall of Fame board of directors who died in 2007. Post's career began during World War II, when he entertained troops in India and Burma before starting his own publishing firm in Los Angeles. He and his first wife, Doree, wrote and recorded many songs for several major labels, and more than one hundred of their songs have been recorded by other artists.

Connie Stevens had a huge hit with their song "Sixteen Reasons" in 1960. "Song for Young Love" was a hit for the Lettermen the same year. Eddie Cochran recorded "Weekend," and Country Music Hall of Famer Don Robertson recorded "Life Goes On."

After Doree's death in 1961, Bill returned to Kansas, where he continued to write and record. His farm near Arkansas City has been turned into a musical museum that has drawn thousands of visitors.

2007

Dawayne Bailey, Manhattan

This guitarist founded the group Rathbone and moved with it to Los Angeles. He left to tour and record as a member of Bob Seger's Silver Bullet Band, playing lead guitar on the *Like a Rock* album. After three years with Seger, he spent nearly a decade with Chicago. In addition to many projects with Chicago, he composed, wrote lyrics, played guitar and was the vocalist on *Chicago XXXII: Stone of Sisyphus*, which was not released until 2008. He joined Veronique Sanson, a popular French performer, for a couple years before settling back in Los Angeles. He continues to work and is signed to the Goblin Girl Label.

Blue Riddim Band, Kansas City

"Around 1975 we started Pat's Blue Riddim Band," drummer and bandleader Steve "Duck" McLane explained. "We were playing 10 percent ska, 10 percent calypso, maybe 25 percent straight-up R&B and the rest of it would be reggae.

People were just everywhere, on top of each other, dancing." Blue Riddim became the first American band to play the Sunsplash Festival in Jamaica.

"We were voted co-'Best Band' of the entire festival," McLane said. "It blew me away that we blew them away. I was expecting pineapples and cantaloupes thrown at us. We're playing these old songs, and we're also from America, and we're also white. It's five o'clock in the morning, and they're going, 'What in the…?'" The original song they played that day, "Nancy Reagan," became a reggae classic. In 1986, the Blue Riddim Band became the first American reggae band of any color to be nominated for a Grammy Award for its live Sunsplash Festival recording.

The Common Few, Chanute

The Common Few started in Chanute in 1964 and played through 1971. The band played a lot of soul music during the early years, mostly in Kansas, Nebraska and Oklahoma. The Common Few was actually the result of the evolution of several earlier incarnations that were short-lived, i.e. the Argonauts, Executers and the Slippers. In 1968, the Common Few recorded its only single, "Love Makes a Man," which received regional recognition.

Marilyn Maye, Wichita and Topeka

Reviewer Rex Reed called Marilyn Maye "just plain miraculous." Included in the ranks of Judy Garland, Frank Sinatra and Billie Holliday, Maye appeared a record seventy-six times on the *Johnny Carson Show*. As a child, she competed for money and prizes in amateur venues in Topeka. She won a thirteen-week appearance on WIBW TV's *B'rer Fox Show*.

"I was 11 years old and every Saturday I sang a song and did a specialty number at the Jayhawk Theater," she explained on her website. "And at the end of every show I sang 'God Bless America.' I think I sang it more than Kate Smith because the show was extended and I sang it for almost two consecutive years!"

While performing at a club in Kansas City, Marilyn was discovered by Steve Allen and became a regular on his show, and there she was discovered by RCA. Recording an album in the Living Room, a New York City club, she was spotted by Ed McMahon, who insisted she perform on the *Tonight Show*. The audience reaction was so tremendous that Johnny Carson extended an open invitation for her to perform whenever she was in town.

Her career has taken her to the stage in *Mame* and *Hello, Dolly!*

Among her numerous awards, including a Grammy nomination, is the 2008 Governor's Arts Award for Distinguished Artist presented by then governor Kathleen Sebelius and the Kansas Arts Commission.

Martina McBride, Wichita

Since her early days singing in her family's country band, to her days with Wichita rock groups, Martina has made a big impression. A multi–platinum selling recording act for RCA, she has sold more than fifteen million records and has been named female vocalist of the year more than once by the ACM and CMA.

Rising Suns, Topeka, Coffeyville and Lawrence

With a more soulful sound than most Topeka bands, the Suns toured extensively. They were named by *Teen Screen* magazine the top act in the Midwest and picked for stardom. After losing most of their equipment in a bus crash, they passed the name on to the Dalton Gang from Coffeyville, who kept the name going after moving to Lawrence. Both versions are included in this nomination.

(Fabulous) Silvertones, Lawrence

Lead singer Roger Calkins made the girls swoon, guitarists credit Frank Plas as an inspiration and drummer Mike Weakley found success later with the Electric Prunes in California.

Tide, Lawrence

Formed in 1968, Tide was led by guitarist Jim Stinger, and it was an eclectic ensemble whose sound incorporated a mix of free jazz, country, blues and

Tide, one of the Mid-Continent bands that toured the Midwest. *Bill Lee and KMHOF collections.*

rock. The band was known for instrumental virtuosity, original compositions and fearless improvisation.

2006

Gene Clark, Kansas City

The late Gene Clark graduated from Bonner Springs High School in the Kansas City area and was a member of several area folk music groups when he was discovered by Randy Sparks of the New Christy Minstrels. After performing with the famed folk group in Los Angeles on two albums, he left the group and resurfaced as one of the founding members of the Byrds. He was the primary songwriter with that group, writing such hits as "I'll Feel a Whole Lot Better." He left in 1966 because he didn't enjoy the demands of traveling with the chart-topping band. In the years following the Byrds, he released many other albums, including *White Light* and his 1974 masterpiece, *No Other*. Around 1987, he began to develop serious health problems, which finally led to his death from a bleeding ulcer in 1991.

Eric & the Norsemen, Lawrence

From the mid-'60s to the early '70s, few bands in Kansas worked the crowds as hard as Eric & the Norsemen. Led by Roger Johnson, they epitomized the garage bands of the era, covering the latest hits with a few original songs thrown into the mix. Entertaining at weekend dances and high school proms, they built a loyal following across the plains.

Melissa Etheridge, Leavenworth

This performer from Leavenworth is one of the state's best-known and most successful musical exports. She picked up a guitar at the age of eight and played in local bands in her teens before attending Berklee College for a year. She then headed to California, getting her first break in 1986 writing the music for the movie *Weeds*. She won Grammy Awards for Best Female Rock Vocal Performance for "Ain't It Heavy" (1992) and "Come to My Window" (1994). "Her recent battle with cancer and her outspokenness on a variety of political topics keeps her in the news, but it's her music that keeps her and her fans going strong," said Bill Lee.

Jerry Hahn, Wichita

This Wichita resident is one of the best jazz guitar players going. He worked with a variety of leading musicians from John Handy and Ginger Baker to Paul Simon and the Fifth Dimension. He became a major name in the 1960s and 1970s for his de facto contribution to the emerging fusion movement and has remained one of its ardent promoters throughout his career. He taught at the Colorado Institute of Art in the early 1990s and joined the faculty of Portland State University in 1995, developing the curriculum for the jazz guitar program. In 2004, Jerry returned to his hometown, Wichita, Kansas, where he continues to perform, record, tour and conduct clinics at Universities and schools.

Kelley Hunt, Lawrence

Kelley Hunt is a regular performer on blues festival stages across the country, and her most recent album made the Top 10 on *Billboard* magazine's blues chart. She is best described as a roots R&B singer/songwriter/piano player and has combined the influences of R&B, roots rock, blues, gospel, folk and soul into her own style and sound. Kelley is also known for her burning boogie-woogie piano style that has become her trademark.

The Jerms, Topeka

Another inductee from the mid-'60s to early-'70s, this Topeka band went through a lot of styles and personnel, but never dropped their quality. The band's leader, Galen Senogles, has been a successful Los Angeles–area record executive, producer and engineer and is now in the film business coordinating the music for both features and television. Other members of the band have performed regularly with the Four Seasons and America.

King Midas & the Muflers, McPherson

The band was organized in 1965, as a four-piece group. In 1966, the group became an eight-piece show band, performing in a six-state area and billed as the King of the Show Bands. The group released several records in the late 1960s, including "Get Down With It" and "Mellow Moonlight." In 2005, the band celebrated forty years together. The group was led by Hall of Fame board member Bob Hapgood, who passed away in 2007. His band mates were honorary pall bearers: Mike Hill, Dennis Frans, Rick Johnson, Scott VanNordstrand, Dale Frans, Bill Wuertz, Steve Zimmerman, Mike D'Amico, Jim Walker, Scott Heitschmidt, Cliff Lambert, Steve Kail, Tom Hapner, Klyd Cunningham, Tom Wheeler, Mike Tinsley, Odel Reed, Richard Collins, Charlie Moyer, Randy Norland, Mark Casebeer, Ron Foulk, Ralph Brown and Mike Badgett.

Spider & the Crabs, Lawrence

This band grew out of Kansas University's Sigma Chi fraternity, and bandleader Steve "Spider" Smith made sure the band was one of the best in Lawrence. With lead singer "Spanky" Landis out front, there was never any doubt. Like many other bands, Spider & the Crabs went through several personnel changes.

Charles "Bud" Ross, Kansas City, 2006 Directors Award

Bud Ross, a bass player and vocalist for Larry Emmett & the Sliders and the Bygones in Kansas City, started a guitar amplifier business in his garage. Tired of blowing out speakers, Ross built the first bass amp that could handle the power to make bass guitars practical rock instruments. His Kustom Electronics outgrew the garage, and Ross moved it to Chanute, Kansas, where it grew to become one of the largest musical equipment companies in the world in the late '60s and early '70s. The distinctive "tuck and roll" upholstery of the amplifiers is remembered fondly by baby boomers. Kustom also developed the first hand-held radars for police to use in catching speeders.

2005

The Blue Things, Hays and Lawrence

The Blue Things (also known as the Bluethings) were a folk-rock and, later, psychedelic band from Lawrence, Kansas (originally from Hays, Kansas), that played from 1964 to 1968, recording one LP and several singles for RCA Records in '66 and '67. The RCA recordings remain their best-known material, although they had previously released singles through Ruff Records, a tiny Texas label. Today, the Blue Things are remembered as one of the best bands to come out of the Midwest in the '60s.

Brewer & Shipley, Kansas City

Brewer & Shipley was a folk rock duo of the late 1960s through 1970s, consisting of singer-songwriters Mike Brewer and Tom Shipley. They were known for their intricate guitar work, vocal harmonies and socially conscious lyrics, which reflected the concerns of their generation, especially the Vietnam War and the struggles for personal and political freedom.

Their biggest hit was the song "One Toke Over the Line" from their 1970 album *Tarkio*. They also had two other singles that made the *Billboard* charts: "Tarkio Road" (1970) and "Shake Off the Demon" (1971). They continue to perform, both separately and together, usually in the Midwest.

Chesmann/Chesmann Square, Kansas City

Chesmann and Chesmann Square were a very popular, longtime Kansas City rock 'n' roll band that played Beatles, Hendrix, Clapton, Stones and soul music in the late '60s and early '70s. They played their last gig in the fall of 1974. The Chesmann combined the musical talents of the three West brothers: Ron, Steve and Gary. Dave Huffines provided lead guitar for the first three years, and Jim McAllister joined the band in 1968 to fill Dave Huffines's spot in the lineup.

Mike Finnigan, Lawrence

The long, lanky Finnigan came to Lawrence from Chicago to play basketball at the University of Kansas. Instead of in the NBA, his professionalism was found on the stage. With soulful vocals and expressive keyboard work, he has been

in constant demand by some of the most respected artists in the business. His distinctive Hammond organ has been featured on recordings or in performances with Jimi Hendrix, Joe Cocker, Etta James, Sam Moore, Crosby Stills and Nash, Dave Mason, Buddy Guy, Manhattan Transfer, Taj Mahal, Michael McDonald, Maria Muldaur, Peter Frampton, Cher, Ringo Starr, Leonard Cohen, Tower

Kelly Finnigan is making a name for himself. At Uncle Bo's in Topeka, he joined his legendary father, Mike, on stage to the delight of the audience. *Karen Knox.*

167

of Power, Rod Stewart, David Coverdale, Tracy Chapman and Destruments. His recording with the group Finnigan & Wood entitled "Crazed Hipsters" is considered a Midwest R&B/rock cult classic. He recorded two solo records in the '70s, one notably with legendary rhythm and blues producer Jerry Wexler. He later collaborated with two other Columbia Artists, Les Dudek and Jim Krueger, with whom he formed DFK (Dudek, Finnegan and Krueger) in 1978. Finnigan continues to tour and perform and is considered by many as one of most soulful vocalists ever.

The Fabulous Flippers, Lawrence

Probably no other single musical group had such an impact on the music of Mid-America in the '60s as the Fabulous Flippers. They were the lead act in the legendary Mid-Continent Productions booking agency owned by John Brown and Mike Murfin. Throughout the Flippers' career, they recorded eight singles, one LP and one EP. They are best remembered for their release on Chicago's Cameo-Parkway Records *Harlem Shuffle/I Don't Want To Cry*. In 1970, the Flippers broke the all-time attendance record at Darlowe Olesen's Roof Garden Ballroom at Lake Okoboji, Iowa. On July 4 of that year, they drew over six thousand teens for a dance, beating the old record of four thousand set in the early '60s by the Everly Brothers.

Kansas, Topeka

Kansas has a history going back more than forty years. With the release of its first major album, *Kansas*, in 1974, Kansas moved into the national music spotlight as a progressive rock band, offering music which combined rock interwoven with classic symphonic tones and complex arrangements. Years later, Kansas is still entertaining crowds of new and old fans with its distinctive, musical style and rich, reflective lyrics. The band's hits include "Carry On Wayward Son" and "Dust in the Wind."

The Red Dogs, Lawrence

In the spring of '65, a band called the Limits was hired to be the house band for the Red Dog Inn in Lawrence and renamed the Red Dogs. The

The Red Dogs were the flagship band of the Red Dog Inn. *Bill Lee and KMHOF collections.*

band played Lawrence monthly and was on the road every weekend plus summer tours. With horns, organ, guitars, drums and well-choreographed routines, the Red Dogs were a terrific and very popular show band. Although they had a Chicago-like structure, they also liked to play music ranging from Lonnie Mack, Jimi Hendrix and Eric Clapton to a James Brown–like revue.

Rodney & the Blazers, Coffeyville

During the first half of the 1960s, when the Beach Boys and the Beatles were bombarding the American charts and rewriting the rules of rock, Kansans Rodney & the Blazers were crossing the country as rock 'n' roll throwbacks, a raucous, wild combo that was more Little Richard than British Invasion and more R&B than pop. They proved to be a very influential midwestern band, employing both a saxophone and a trumpet (expanded into a full horn section later in the decade by admitted fans Chicago) and touring as one of the first truly biracial aggregates. Bass player Rodney Lay Sr. and drummer Bob York kicked around together in a band known as the Off Beats throughout the last couple years of the 1950s. By 1960, with the addition of Bob "Sir Robert" Scott on saxophone and Pete "Peaches" Williams on guitar, they had transformed themselves into Rodney & the Blazers, named after their habit of wearing blazers instead of normal jackets for their stage show. It wasn't their only idiosyncrasy in appearance—they also dyed their hair silver and wore sunglasses onstage. Don Downing was soon added on piano, as well as sharing lead vocals with Lay, and they were soon playing regular gigs every Friday night at the El Rancho Opera House located between their Coffeyville hometown and Independence, Kansas. That summer, they recorded and released their first single, "Teenage Cinderella," on their own Kampus label, which became a number-one hit in several large markets around the country.

Big Joe Turner, Kansas City

Big Joe Turner (born Joseph Vernon Turner Jr. on May 18, 1911[?]) was an American blues shouter from Kansas City, Missouri. According to the songwriter Doc Pomus, "Rock and roll would have never happened without him." Although he came to his greatest fame in the 1950s with his pioneering rock 'n' roll recordings, particularly "Shake, Rattle and Roll," Turner's career as a performer stretched from the 1920s into the 1980s.

John Brown and Mike Murfin, 2005 Directors Award

John Brown and Mike Murfin opened the Red Dog Inn in Lawrence, Kansas, on January 1, 1965. They started Mid Continent Productions in the mid-'60s and built it into one of the most successful booking and management agencies of all time. Brown and Murfin helped form and, in some respects, create such groups as the Fabulous Flippers, the Red Dogs, the Blue Things, the Young Raiders, the Rising Suns and Spider & the Crabs. Their radio ads on fifty-thousand-watt KOMA in Oklahoma City reached what has been estimated at three million listeners per night all the way from Oklahoma to the Canadian border.

Louis and Betty Blasco and "My Happiness:" The Story of a Standard

By Allen Blasco

Louis Blasco and Betty Peterson were both graduates of Northeast High School, alma mater to many famous Kansas Citians. However, they never met until both went to work for Jenkins Music. Jenkins was once a midwestern dynasty, with stores spanning five states and dealing in all things musical. The backbone of the Jenkins empire was a thriving music publishing division, which Louis Blasco managed and built from the ground up, choosing for publication such soon-to-be-classics as "Twelfth Street Rag," "Trouble in Mind" and "Just Because." Mr. Blasco was also a fine musician and played in the Coon-Sanders Nighthawks, an early Kansas City Jazz band. His eye for talent convinced Dave Kapp, head of Decca Records, to sign two then unknown artists: Count Basie and the Andrew Sisters. But it was his golden ear for hit songs that gave him the sobriquet "Mr. Music of the Midwest."

A few years after their marriage in 1943, Lou and Betty Blasco were in the process of leaving Jenkins, having decided to go into the music publishing business for themselves. Lou had with him the melody to a song written fifteen years earlier by local bandleader Borney Bergantine. In 1947, he asked his wife to write lyrics for the song, using her maiden name of Betty Peterson. A talented singer and songwriter in her own right, she had no trouble complying. In December of that year, Lou supervised a recording of the song by husband-and-wife duo Jon and Sondra Steele at a studio owned by Vic Damon, two floors down from his own office in the Midland Building on Twelfth and Baltimore Streets. A forgettable novelty song was recorded for the other side of the record. When RCA, Decca and all the other major labels refused to buy the master, Lou convinced the studio owner

The first version of Stonewall with (left to right) Kenny Mairs, Greg Whitfield and Allen Blasco. The band changed personnel but performed for eight years. Allen had just left the Clergymen, where he "earned his chops," getting the vocals that would enable him to lead Stonewall. *Courtesy Allen Blasco.*

to release the record on his own self-named Damon label. The problem was he was pushing the forgettable novelty tune as the "A" side. When a disc jockey in Pittsburgh, Pennsylvania, flipped the record and played the "B" side, it took off like the proverbial rocket. That song, "My Happiness," would spend fifteen weeks during 1948 in the Top 10, spawning multiple versions by artists such as Ella Fitzgerald and the Pied Pipers, which also became Top 10 hits that same year. *Cashbox* magazine, a music industry publication, gave "My Happiness" its coveted Song of the Year award for 1948.

Lou started his own record label, Cardinal Records, bringing his brother Frank on board as vice-president. The label's first release was the debut recording of Arkansas native Jimmie Driftwood. An American folk music scholar, he is best remembered for writing "The Battle of New Orleans," a massive hit for Johnny Horton in 1959. Other artists who recorded for Cardinal include the Mulcays, Kansas City saxophone legend Big Bob Dougherty and a young lady from Oklahoma named Colleen Carroll.

"No Tellin'" and "Blue Bonnet Waltz" were the first of a handful of singles she recorded for a number of small labels. Her career as a country singer never got off the ground, but her son, a gentleman named Garth Brooks, eventually did pretty well for himself.

As if their plates weren't full enough, Lou and Betty also formed Blasco Artists Bureau, a talent management and booking agency. Kansas City was a highly segregated town in the late 1940s and early 1950s. Vocalist Myra Taylor and pianist/vocalist Joshua Johnson were but two of many African American artists on the roster. The Blascos successfully booked them and others in upscale whites-only establishments, receiving death threats and hate mail in the process. This pioneering effort at desegregation broke the so-called color barrier in Kansas City for the first time, at least as far as entertainment was concerned.

Another barrier of sorts was broken in 1950 when the Blascos, with royalties from the success of "My Happiness," decided to build their dream house in the newly incorporated Johnson County suburb of Leawood, Kansas. Though the Leawood city charter of the time had racial covenants that banned virtually every minority group imaginable, Lou Blasco's Italian American heritage was conveniently overlooked by the city fathers, and construction began in the spring of 1951.

Meanwhile, the success of "My Happiness" was changing the way the record industry did business. "This was the first record on an independent label to really make it big," said Jon Steele in a front-page *Kansas City Times* article from 1977.

"Before, the industry was dominated by RCA, Capitol, Columbia, and Decca. And suddenly, a little outfit called Damon Records in Kansas City had the song that was number one for fifteen weeks. It showed that independent labels could make it." And make it they did. Labels with names like Ace, Chance, Chess, Modern and Vee Jay started having hits with a driving new danceable sound that was soon to be called rock 'n' roll. Parents, along with music industry insiders, watched in dismay while children of the postwar era quickly adopted this new sound as their own. Initially, the mainstream record industry was completely caught off guard, having no understanding of the music, let alone how to sell it to a huge new youth market, eventually christened the baby boomers. Over time, the so-called major labels would have success in this strange new musical world not of their own making, but essentially, they'd be playing catch-up ball with this new sound well into the next decade. It was the rise of this new music on independent labels that spawned and sustained the nascent rock 'n' roll era. One of those independent labels was Sun Records out of Memphis, Tennessee. Label owner and engineer Sam Phillips had a side business called the Memphis Recording Service, where anyone with $3.98 plus tax could come in and make a demonstration record. On Saturday, July 18, 1953, an eighteen-year-old truck driver named Elvis Presley did just that, choosing his mother's favorite song, "My Happiness," as his first ever recording.

At that time, Elvis was still a few years away from immortality, and the Blascos had no way of knowing "the king" of something called "rock 'n' roll" was about to launch his storied reign with a demo of their song. Betty would live to see its eventual release in 1990, and she even met an appreciative Elvis in Kansas City during his breakthrough tour of 1956. Sadly, Lou would not. A trip to the Mayo Clinic revealed that Lou had cancer. "Mr. Music of the Midwest" passed away on March 17, 1954, leaving a wife, two small children and an impressive musical and personal legacy that continues to this day.

"My Happiness" became a massive hit for Connie Francis in 1958–59, cementing her status as "America's Sweetheart of

Song," and one of pop music's top female vocalist of all time. Over the years, "My Happiness" has continued to be recorded by hundreds of artists as diverse as Bing Crosby, Jim Reeves, Fats Domino, Frank Sinatra, Arthur "Guitar Boogie" Smith and Chris Isaak, to name just a few. Betty celebrated most all of these, and on March 3, 2006, at age eighty-seven, she passed away peacefully in her sleep. The classic lyric she wrote for a timeless melody remains a lasting gift of happiness for music lovers the world over.

On March 22, 2008, at Liberty Hall in Lawrence Kansas, Louis O. Blasco and Betty Peterson Blasco were inducted into the Kansas Music Hall of Fame.

EPILOGUE

THE STRAIGHT ROAD

My landscape has changed. Instead of the crooked road, the roads these days are almost perfectly straight, heading right into the horizon, to the rising sun, to Texas and to the Dakotas. The directions are sharp and defined, not softened by deep woods or obscured by hairpin curves.

One musician described his memories of the road. The band bus would arrive in a small town in western Kansas and set up in the local park or armory or high school gym, whatever would accommodate a crowd. Near dark on those summer and fall days, often during the harvest season when farmers were wrenching every moment of light from the day, the fans would come. Like Custer's cavalry, they could be seen by the clouds of dust they were kicking up on the road. From every direction, the line of cars and pickups were headed to the place they could kick back or kick up and leave the dusty, ordinary world.

It was the same for the bands who traveled with military or who played in Dodge City's crowded halls as it is for the band Kansas that continues to tour the world with semis carrying its equipment. It is about creating an experience that transcends the mundane. These musicians do that every day.

Performing, especially on stage with the applause and energy it creates, can be heady stuff. It is easy for the egos to get out of line. What has struck me again and again since moving to the Sunflower State is the incredible absence of self-importance and inflated egos, even among those who have achieved great success and, on occasion, even greatness.

When the Kansas Hall of Fame was preparing for the induction ceremony in 2013, I shared many e-mails and a few conversations with

Musician and guitar store owner Rick Roberts is a regular with Mark and the Sharks and often joins other bands who come to Topeka to perform. *Doug Ruth*.

Harry Muldrow has entertained audiences for decades, whether as a member of a band, as a solo act or hosting jams. *Noel Coalson*.

the band's drummer, Phil Ehart. Phil continues to perform and is also the group's manager. He is conscientious. He asked what the order of induction would be at the ceremony, having been around these events long enough to know that the last honored is the *most* honored. I told him that it was under discussion at that moment, and of course, it had been suggested that Kansas be last up. Also inducted in 2013 was the First Kansas Colored Infantry, a military unit with many former slaves who organized, fought and died before the passage of the Emancipation Proclamation. General Roosevelt Barfield, also a native Kansan, flew in from Washington to accept the award on the infantry's behalf. Phil was adamant that it be the most honored.

"I am speaking for myself and the rest of the band in saying we would be very uncomfortable in being honored above men who died for their country," he told me. "We are just a rock 'n' roll band."

While millions of fans worldwide might have thought differently, Phil does speak for the band in that respect. The band members are grateful to have been successful doing what they love. There are many talented musicians and artists who cannot say the same. Whatever the venue, whatever the accolades, their feet remain firmly planted in the soil of Kansas.

Humility and generosity are the common threads in the diverse musical scene. If the hours that these people donated to causes could suddenly be compensated, Kansas would be a state full of millionaires. Just the other night, I ran into Joel Edison, already serving above and beyond in all his efforts with the annual Jam4Dan. He was checking out the venue for a fundraiser he is organizing for a little girl with cancer. His day job is with Manning Music, but his super-hero cape is on around the clock.

In Kansas, this generosity is not rare. Perhaps it is not rare in other parts of the world either, but in Kansas, with a population of a little under three million spread out over nearly eighty-two thousand acres, you notice. Kyler Carpenter came to Topeka from Larned to be the children's program coordinator at the Topeka Shawnee County Public Library. He is the most popular person there, but he goes so far beyond those walls of the library. The jam he hosts at the neighborhood bar, Speck's, on Sunday evenings is a training ground for aspiring musicians from two years old and up. He encourages and cajoles but gets lots of other musicians to give of their time and talents as well. In the not too distant future, you will be watching a young star on television who is saying, "It all began with Kyler Carpenter at Speck's Bar & Grill."

Orin Friesen is another busy man who somehow finds time for his favorite causes. When the Home on the Range Cabin needed attention and financial

Jerry Reiman pays a tribute to Civil War veterans in Historic Topeka Cemetery. *Author's collection.*

support, it was Orin who organized a fundraiser with his friend Michael Martin Murphey headlining the event. Murph, too, has an incredible heart but is so in demand it says much for this project and his friendship with Orin that he lent his time and talent to this cause.

Another word that is tossed about is genius, and in Kansas, it's not that rare. Kerry Livgren and Andy McKee come immediately to mind. Kerry's vision guided the band Kansas into new and uncharted waters, literally, *To the Point of Know Return*. Likewise, Andy Mckee has done things with a guitar that simply were not done before—well, except maybe for Pat Matheny. This guy must roll out of bed in the morning wondering which award will come his way today. He truly defies classification. Kirke Mechem has turned Kansas history into opera with *John Brown*, a stunning accomplishment in bringing together those turbulent times in history and making musical sense of them.

I have come to the conclusion after my years in Kansas that it, too, has a soundtrack. But it is so many different types of music. Yes, I found the old time that my uncle Tommy Jarrell would have loved with the Euphoria String Band, but I also found Mike Finnigan. There's the bluegrass with fine groups like Pastense, and there's blues with Josh Vowell. There's jazz,

Judy Coder takes cowboy, and girl, music to audiences around the world. *Courtesy Judy Coder.*

classical and New Age. My friend Judy Coder sings, writes and yodels and has the prettiest clothes of any cowgirl you ever saw! She has taken Kansas to fans throughout the United States and Europe.

Many events celebrate many genres: the Sunflower Music Festival at Washburn University, the symphony in the Flint Hills, the Country Stampede and the dozens, if not hundreds, of smaller events throughout the state. Many reflect the ethnicities of their homeland, like Fiesta Mexicana in Topeka or the Kansas City Irish Fest. German and Czech communities make traditional music a part of every celebration. In Lindsborg, settled by the Swedes, Bethany College hosts the Messiah Festival of Music and Art during Holy Week. Messiah Festival of the Arts is the longest-running performances of Handel's *Messiah* in North America, having begun in 1882. Music was a very real link to the home left behind, and it made the new environment feel like home.

The Jammen Souls perform at the Fiesta Mexicana. Band members include Sam Herchberger, Steve Sepulveda, Joe Rocha, Jim Davis, David Hughes and Victor Rodriguez. *Louise Neal Pedrosa.*

Bill Lynch (left) and Rick Moors came in from Los Angeles to perform at the Bottleneck in Lawrence. *Deb Bisel.*

It has worked for me.

Radio personality and performer Kim Murphree (inducted into the KMHOF with the Exceptions) spoke of the ways in which she has been blessed by music:

> *My life in music has given me great friends, great memories and great knowledge. Music has given me the opportunity to understand communication beyond human speech. On stage or off, between band members and with audience members, music eliminated the walls between individuals and created a shared experience with joy, laughter, tears and triumph. So much more than any one song…or any one gig…a life tuned to melodies and memories and the honor of being numbered among the finest musicians in my home state in the Kansas Music Hall of Fame—I cannot imagine anything better. Music anchors my life to weather any storm. I sing with a grateful heart.*

Kansas is not widely thought of as a state full of creative people, but it absolutely is. It is a diverse landscape with people of all ethnicities and backgrounds, and there is a wonderful creative energy throughout. What is also common from one corner of the state to the other is the generous spirit that fosters the creative spirit. If you listen closely, you can hear it in the south wind.

INDEX

ABOUT THE AUTHOR

Debra Goodrich Bisel speaks to hundreds of groups around the country and has appeared in numerous documentaries, most recently, Lone Chimney Films' *Road to Valhalla* and *Gunslingers* on the American Heroes Channel. She is the resident historian at Historic Topeka Cemetery, where she oversees fundraising and programming. She is co-host of the weekly TV show *Around Kansas*, a feature of AgAmInKansas. Her co-host, Frank Chaffin, is a longtime radio person and is a partner in the Internet reincarnation of WREN. He counts among his friends Randy Sparks, of the New Christy Minstrels, who wrote and performed the theme song for *Around Kansas*.

She speaks to groups throughout the nation on various history topics, including Vice President Charles Curtis, who was descended from the Kaw and the Osage, and the Civil War's First Ladies. The

Frank Chaffin and Deb Bisel share hosting duties on the weekly TV show *Around Kansas. Heather Silver Newell.*

thinly disguised Deb Goodman, a character inspired by Deb, is the intended murder victim in Esther Luttrell's latest mystery, *Murder in Magenta*.

This is Deb's third book with The History Press and her first foray into the world of music.

Visit us at
www.historypress.net
....

This title is also available as an e-book